The Dragon of Kinabalu
and other Borneo stories

The Dragon of Kinabalu
and other Borneo stories

OWEN RUTTER
F.R.G.S., F.R.A.I.

Natural History Publications (Borneo)
Kota Kinabalu

1999

Published by

Natural History Publications (Borneo) Sdn. Bhd.
A913, 9th Floor, Wisma Merdeka
P.O. Box 13908
88846 Kota Kinabalu, Sabah, Malaysia
Tel: 088-233098 Fax: 088-240768
e-mail: chewlun@tm.net.my

First published 1930, by Clement Ingleby, London

This abridged edition published in 1999 by
Natural History Publications (Borneo) Sdn. Bhd.
Kota Kinabalu, Sabah, Malaysia

The Dragon of Kinabalu
    and other Borneo Stories
    by Owen Rutter

Perpustakaan Negara Malaysia   Cataloguing-in-Publication Data

Rutter, Owen, 1899–
    The dragon of Kinabalu / Owen Rutter.
    ISBN 983-812-020-0
    1. Tales—Sabah. 2. Folk Literature—Sabah. I. Title.
    398.20959521

Printed in Malaysia

To

DESMOND MOUNTJOY

FOR WHOM LIFE IS
(AS IT SHOULD BE)
A FAIRY TALE
I DEDICATE THESE STORIES
FROM A GARDEN OF THE SUN

Contents

Preface ix

The Dragon of Kinabalu 1

The King of Crocodiles 9

The Geruda Bird 17

The Felling of Tinagat Rock 24

The Spectral Huntsman 31

The Enchanted Basket and the Lazy Woman 37

The Vampires of Tempassuk 45

The Cunning Mousedeer 52

The Orang's Bride 60

The Princess from under the Lake 67

The Magic Beanstalk 75

The Bewitched Goat 85

The Tree of Echoes 91

The Vengeance of the Bog 97

Preface

Most of these tales have been told me, at one time or another, by those good friends of mine, the brown people who live upon the sunny plains or in the forest uplands of North Borneo. One would make shorter a ride through the jungle along a path that wound mazily about the hills; one would help to pass an evening in a long house up-country, when all but the circle of the fire was deep in shadow; another brings back a picture of a native boat beneath the moon, my helmsman breaking off his story to whistle for the wind to fill our great square sail. And I sometimes think that perhaps I came to hear them because I was always ready to believe that every one of them was true.

Some, particularly *The Spectral Huntsman* and *The Cunning Mousedeer*, are common to all Malayan folk-lore; others belong more peculiarly to Borneo. They have been handed down from the grim days of piracy and head-hunting, but those who remember them now live at peace, with a philosophy as sound as any in the world (for their wants are few) and with a prospect, if the best influences of the West reach them without the worst, of even happier and more prosperous days to come.

O.R.

The Dragon of Kinabalu.

The Dragon of Kinabalu

One of the Emperors of China, who lived many centuries ago, had three sons, each of whom was very jealous of the other. In fact, so great was their rivalry for power, that the Emperor was at a loss to decide which of them to appoint as his successor, for he feared that the son who ascended the throne would be done to death by his disappointed brothers.

While he was turning the problem over in his mind, a traveller from the island of Borneo arrived at the Court with tales of a marvellous carbuncle that was guarded by a gigantic dragon on the mountain of Kinabalu, which cast its shadow over that distant land. This dragon made his home, the traveller said, in a great lake upon the very summit of the mountain, and, unless attacked, would only emerge on nights when the moon was full. Then he would lie playing with his carbuncle, which was as red as a sunset and as large as a peacock's egg, tossing it up into the air, like a child with a ball, and catching it again in his mouth.

The Emperor, who loved everything that was strange and beautiful, burnt to possess this precious jewel, and, as he listened to the traveller's story, it seemed to him that the carbuncle might well help to solve the problem of the jealous sons. Accordingly he summoned them to his presence and set them a quest.

"My sons," said he, "as you are well aware, which of you to appoint as my successor to the throne is a problem that has long perplexed me. Now I have it in my mind to set you a quest. This is my decree: I will give my Empire to whomsoever of you shall take the jewel from the dragon of Kinabalu and deliver it into my hands. But the penalty for failure shall be death."

The brothers accepted their father's decree without demur.

Kwun Wang, the eldest son, by virtue of his birth, was allowed to try his fortune first, and he set sail for Borneo with a great fleet of tongkongs and a host of followers.

In those times Kinabalu was much nearer the sea than it is to-day, and, when they had reached the northern coast of Borneo, the prince and his followers had not far to go before they came to the mountain's foot. But they found to their dismay that its sheer rocky sides towered towards the sky almost as steeply as a column, and every time they made attempts to clamber to the top the dragon rose from his lair in the lake and wrought such havoc amongst them that those who were not killed fled in confusion, leaving the precious carbuncle in its resting-place.

Meanwhile the Emperor's second son, Sun Wang, hearing no news of the expedition, resolved to try his fortune too. He also set out with a great fleet and an army of retainers, but, for all that, he met with no better success than his brother, and hundreds of his people were hurled down the steep mountain-side by the infuriated dragon and lost their lives.

Both the brothers grieved bitterly at their failure, and it seemed to them that they must remain for ever as exiles in that lonely land, for they dared not return to China without the object of the quest, knowing that their father would most certainly keep his word and would order them to be beheaded without delay.

To make matters worse, a great storm arose and sank their ships before their eyes as they stood upon the shore; after that there was nothing for it but to eke out a miserable existence in the Borneo jungles with those of their followers who still remained. They were beset by dangers, for in the forests dwelt savage head-hunters who were ever on the alert to creep behind them from tree to tree as they marched along a jungle track; if one of them chanced to straggle by the way, a little brown man would leap out upon him and, with one great sweep of his hair-bedecked knife, would sever the head of the luckless Chinese and bear it home triumphantly to his village in the hills. Thence, for many nights afterwards, would come sounds of riot and rejoicing as the wild men celebrated their victory with dance and song.

To the minds of the Chinese, too, other dangers even more terrible lurked in the forest, for to them it seemed peopled, not only by implacable head-hunters, but also by mysterious spirits and misshapen goblins, who would inflict torture and death more ghastly than that dealt by any human hand. Moreover, if any of them was unwary enough to stray towards the mountain-side, their enemy the dragon, ever watchful, never failed to slay him with one blow from monstrous tail or wing.

In time, however, they became more cautious and made a little clearing on the banks of a pebbly river; round it they built a palisade of pointed stakes and, within, each man set to and prepared the land for the rice-seed he had brought with him from China. Every Chinese loves his garden, and the only happiness that came to the exiles in those weary days was in watching the young shoots growing, as green as grass-snakes; for there is no more beautiful colour in all the world than that of rice when it is pushing its way into the sunlight through the smooth sheet of shining water that covers the mud in which it grows.

In this way they lived, without ever being able to send a message to their native land. At last, after many months had passed and nothing had been heard at the Imperial Court of the two adventurers, Kong Wang, the youngest of the three sons, decided that it was time he started upon the quest himself. Instead of taking with him a large retinue like his brother, however, he filled his ships with thousands of great iron cauldrons, "for," thought he, "if this mountain is as steep as the traveller says, we shall need stairs to climb it."

When he reached Borneo he found his brothers disconsolate

at their misfortunes, and they urged him to abandon so foolhardy an adventure.

"How can you, with nothing but your cauldrons, expect to fare better than we and all our men have fared?" said they. "Better by far that we should embark in the ships that you have brought and return forthwith to China. Once there, we can fling ourselves at our father's feet and all three implore his mercy."

"Nay, brother," answered Kong Wang stoutly, "surely you would think little of me were I to abandon the quest so faintheartedly as that. I too must try to capture the plaything from the dragon's mouth."

With that he bade his men bring the cauldrons from the tongkongs' holds. These he set one upon the other, leaning them against the sheer mountain-side and, having chosen a night when the moon was full, by this means succeeded in climbing up alone and reaching the summit of Kinabalu, his only weapon a ball of red-hot iron which he carried in his right hand.

It was a cloudless night, and in the moonlight Kong Wang could see the dragon sitting upon a crag beside the lake, playing with a carbuncle as red as a sunset and as large as a peacock's egg, just as the traveller had told. Its body was covered with scales of mossy green, and as it moved to and fro its bony wings scraped noisily against the rock, while its sinuous tail flicked fitfully from side to side like that of a cat about to spring. A great barbed tongue lolled from its hideous mouth when the carbuncle was in the air, but even more terrifying were its eyes, which seemed like two pools of swampy water on which the sun is shining, so dark and mysterious were they and so strange the lights which flashed out from their depths.

For a few moments Kong Wang crouched spellbound upon the rocky ledge, then, plucking up his courage and using one of the cauldrons as a shield, he crept stealthily forward and, as the dragon threw the carbuncle up into the air, flung the fiery ball of iron full in the monster's face. The guardian of the mountain was so taken aback by this sudden onslaught that he forgot to catch the jewel in his mouth again, and instead he sought refuge in his lake, leaving the carbuncle gleaming upon the ground.

Eagerly Kong Wang seized the prize he had come so far to find, and climbed down the cauldron staircase with all the speed he could. He reached the mountain's foot in safety, and in a few moments the news had spread to the camp that the carbuncle had been taken.

Immediately all was confusion. Helter-skelter Kong Wang and his brothers, together with all their followers, rushed down to the ships. They set sail in haste. Once they were upon the high seas, they thought, they would be safe.

But, long before they were out of sight of Kinabalu's peaks, the outraged dragon recovered from his fright and came after them in hot pursuit. Many of the ships he capsized with blows from his wings or from his lashing tail, and at last (so furious was he) one of them he swallowed whole, crew and all. This was his undoing, for the great tongkong made him so heavy that he could no longer swim, much less fly, and, amidst wild churning and splashing of the water, he sank writhing to the bottom of the sea.

By this time, however, all the other ships save that in which the three brothers had sought refuge were sinking; many of the crews and of the princes' followers were drowned, and those who succeeded in gaining the shore again had no means of reaching their native land, so they settled in the jungle country for good and all, and formed a little colony of their own, taking their wives from the women of the head-hunters, with whom they at length made peace.

In the meantime the tongkong of the three princes, having escaped the onslaughts of the dragon, eventually drew near the shores of China, but it was with mixed feelings that the two elder brothers saw the crinkled coast-line of their country, for they knew that they had failed in the quest, and that their heads would pay the penalty.

At length Kwun Wang hit upon a scheme whereby he might save his life, and, with honeyed words, he induced his young brother to entrust the jewel to his safe keeping. Then, as soon as the ship had cast anchor, he made his way hurriedly to the Imperial Palace and laid the long-desired carbuncle at his father's feet.

"You have done well, my son," said the Emperor, "my throne and empire shall be yours. As for your brothers, even as I pledged my word, they shall pay the penalty, and tomorrow's sun shall see their heads rolling upon the ground."

Kwun Wang left his father's presence well pleased with his subtlety, for having, as he thought, saved his own life he cared little what became of his brothers. But before sunset Kong Wang, eluding the guards who had gone in search of him, came also to the Palace, and obtained admittance to the Emperor's audience-chamber, nor was it long before he convinced his father that he and no other had secured the carbuncle of Kinabalu from the dragon's mouth.

The Emperor was furious when he found how nearly he had been duped by his own son and immediately gave orders for the arrest of Kwun Wang, but he, learning that his plot had failed, set sail in a fast tongkong and escaped, followed by his brother Sun Wang in another. The course they set was south, but a great storm arose during which the two ships became separated. Kwun Wang's tongkong was blown to the shores of the Malay Peninsula and wrecked upon the rocky coast, but that of Sun Wang, after many adventures, reached the river town of Brunei, where, from time immemorial, had dwelt the Rajahs of Borneo in a palm-leaf palace built on posts above the water.

At the moment of Sun Wang's arrival it so happened that Brunei was without a ruler and torn with contending factions, one of which offered him the throne. Sun Wang, a prince without a country, asked nothing more, and, having overthrown the enemies of those who had besought his aid, he founded a new dynasty in Brunei and never again revisited his native land, while, as a proof that this tale is true, they say that to this day you may see the great carbuncle, as red as a sunset and as large as a peacock's egg, in the Imperial Palace of the Son of Heaven at Peking.

He found himself in a noble place.

The King of the Crocodiles

Long ago, in the district of Papar, lived a very old man called Bangsat, who was famed throughout the land for his skill in medicine and for the manner in which he could mix healing potions and make magic charms. One evening, as the sun was setting across the shining rice-fields, Bangsat was taking a stroll along the banks of the muddy Papar River when he heard someone stirring in a clump of bamboo near by, and a voice said:

"Bangsat, I want your help."

Bangsat looked round and discovered an old man, who was weeping bitterly.

"What is the matter?" he asked, drawing nearer, "and how is it that you call me for help?"

"Alas!" cried the old man, "my daughter is at the point of death. She is being choked by a fish-bone that has stuck in her throat, and no one in all my kingdom can get it out. I have heard that you are skilled in medicine, and if you will but help us and save her life, I will give you as much gold as you can carry away from my palace."

Bangsat pricked up his ears as soon as he heard the old man speak of his palace, and began to wonder who on earth the stranger could be. Anyhow, whoever he was, the chance of getting such a fat fee seemed too good to be lost, and so he agreed without demur to give his services.

"Is it far from here?" he asked.

"No," replied the other, "and I myself will be your horse." Whereupon, without more ado, the old man changed himself into a crocodile; and before the astonished Bangsat had time to run away he heard the same voice saying:

"You need not be frightened, Bangsat, for I swear no harm shall come to you. Only sit on my back and trust yourself to me, and I will take you safely to my palace beneath the river. I am the King of the Crocodiles."

"But my medicine will be of no use to a crocodile," protested Bangsat, "and how can I live under the water? If I come with you most surely I shall be drowned."

"First of all," replied the crocodile, "you must know that when we crocodiles are in our homes we are human beings like you and your people, and that we only take this reptile form when we swim in the river or lie basking upon its banks. As to your journey under the water: I will see to that. Is it likely that I should want a dead doctor to heal my daughter?"

These arguments seemed fairly specious ones to Bangsat; moreover, although he did not greatly care about the business, he was a greedy old man, and the prospect of getting so much gold overcame his lingering fears. He thought how he would never have to do any more work, but instead would be able to squat always by his open doorway, smoking and chewing betel-nut, or to sit in the coffee-shops as long and as often as he wished, drinking and gossiping with his friends. So at last he jumped on to the crocodile's back, clinging to the scaly hide as best he could. The yellow waters of the river closed over him, but before he knew where he was he found himself in a noble palace with marble floors and walls hung with richest tapestries. Everywhere he looked he saw ancient jars adorned with dragons, brasswork which he knew must be hundreds of years old and beyond price, weapons whose hilts and sheaths were inlaid with gold and precious stones. It was a palace worthy of a king, and Bangsat's heart bounded as he thought that some of the wealth he saw would be his before he left for the upper world again.

The Crocodile King bade Bangsat wait for a few moments in the great entrance hall of the palace. While he was looking about him and working out in his mind what each treasure he saw was worth, two more crocodiles came in and, without taking any notice of him, entered a chamber off the main hall. A minute or two later there sallied forth two men dressed in silken sarongs—the skirt which in Malaya both men and women wear—and cloth-of-gold with jewelled turbans upon their heads and jewelled weapons at their sides.

Bangsat's curiosity got the better of him, and, creeping to the doorway, he peeped into the room. The sight that met his eyes made him jump back in astonishment, for there from the pegs on the walls hung rows and rows of crocodiles' skins. At that moment another crocodile hurried past him; standing on its hind legs it shook itself three times, whereupon the reptile was transformed into a mortal, gorgeously attired like those Bangsat had just seen. This splendid being, without the least concern, stooped down, picked up the skin, hung it upon a vacant peg and sauntered out by the way that he had come.

Before Bangsat had time to recover from his surprise the King returned, having himself shed his skin; once more he was a wizened old man, but dressed in all the splendour of an Eastern potentate. With him was his son, who led the way to a room where, upon a divan covered with mats of woven colours, lay a beautiful maiden clad only in a sarong. Her eyes were closed and she was moaning pitifully; her breath was coming in little gasps, and she kept clutching at her throat as if in direst agony.

Bangsat approached the bed and examined the girl, who was no other than the daughter of the King. There was undoubtedly something in her throat, he found, but it seemed too long to be a fish-bone. Keeping her mouth open with one hand he put the first finger and the thumb of the other down the damsel's throat and drew forth, not a fish-bone, but a golden hairpin.

If you should ever chance to raise the cover from a morning breakfast-dish and find beneath it, instead of the expected kidneys, a human head, you could not be more unpleasantly surprised than Bangsat was, for he recognized the pin as one belonging to a village girl who had disappeared mysteriously a few days before while she was bathing in the river. He was, however, one of those who have attained sufficient wisdom in life to realize that what the eye makes up its mind not to see the heart does not grieve over. He felt that the King was watching him narrowly, and with an effort he recovered his presence of mind.

"As you surmised, Your Majesty," he said gravely, "a fishbone. I think you will find now that Her Royal Highness will have relief."

The King, delighted with Bangsat's skill no less than with his good sense, then led the way to the royal treasure-chamber. There Bangsat's gaze feasted upon gold and precious stones such as he had never seen before. His eyes glistened.

"Take what you will," said the King, "for so high a service demands reward as high."

Bangsat did not need to be told twice, and he undid the cloth which he wore about his head as a protection against the sun, and in it tied up as much gold as it would contain, cramming a few more handfuls into such pockets as he possessed, and even filling his tobacco-box and his hollow bamboo pipe.

Both the King and his son pressed him to stay on for a few more days in the palace, but Bangsat, not unmindful of the skins he had seen hanging on their pegs, thought it might be as well to get away whilst he could, so he made an excuse that his wife would be getting anxious about him and said he must be gone. As a parting gift, the King presented him with a Malayan sword, the wavy blade of which was cunningly damascened and inscribed with texts from the Koran, the hilt inlaid with gold and rubies; then, having summoned a slave to bring him his skin, he transformed himself again, bade Bangsat jump on his back a second time and bore him to the upper world. On the banks of the river they parted, and once more the King of the

Crocodiles gave Bangsat his thanks.

"You have rendered the crocodiles a great service," he said graciously, "and as long as you keep their secret they will always remain your friends. But beware that you say not a word of what you have seen to your own people, or it may go ill with you indeed."

Bangsat was in such a hurry to get away that he would have promised anything, and, having assured the King that he would never breathe a word of the adventures which had befallen him, he made off towards his village. It was not until he was climbing up the ladder of his little palm-leaf house that it struck him that he would have to explain to his wife and to the village chief whence had come the jewelled sword and the hoard of gold with which he returned. For a long time he evaded all questions, and then tried to silence them by saying that he had found the treasures in a forgotten hollow on a hillside, the remains of a grave of long ago. The chief, however, at once asked to be taken to the spot, and eventually, tiring of his eternal questions, Bangsat, with many injunctions to secrecy, blurted out the whole story.

Tabiko, the village chief, was highly delighted when he heard of the wealth of the crocodiles, for, as the King had a son, he thought he saw his way to getting a handsome dowry for his daughter, who was still unmarried. Like Bangsat, he was influenced by motives of personal greed, since in Borneo a prospective bridegroom has to pay the dowry over to the father of the girl he wishes to marry, and the old gentleman usually keeps it for himself. In fact, to Tabiko it seemed a splendid opportunity to retrieve the family fortunes, which had fallen on evil days, for so poor was he become that all his valuables had long since found their way to the local pawnshop, all, that is, except one brass rice-measure, which had been handed down from father to son for generations.

Saying nothing of his plans, he made Bangsat describe the

King of the Crocodiles as he appeared in the guise of an old man, and spent the next few evenings wandering along the river bank. On the fourth night he met the King, who had assumed his human form and was taking an evening stroll. Tabiko passed the time of day and they stopped for a few moments to chat about the harvest and the price of buffaloes. After that they often met again, and at length grew so friendly that one night, when Bangsat was away on a visit to another village, Tabiko invited the King to his house, where he took care that his daughter should be, dressed in the most splendid clothes the family could produce. Her beauty made an obvious impression upon the King, and after he had paid several visits to Tabiko's house he asked her hand in marriage for his son.

Matters were going exactly as Tabiko had planned, and he smiled indulgently when the King said:

"My village is far away at the head of the river, but I will bring my son here if you will agree to the marriage."

"Very well," answered Tabiko, who characteristically did not ask his daughter whether she had any objection to marrying a crocodile, "but the dowry must be this brass measure filled with gold." And he pointed to the family rice-measure, which was standing upon a box inside the doorway.

To this the King agreed willingly. A few days later he and his son appeared, bringing many presents of silken sarongs and ornaments and brass and a large supply of gold. But when the gold was poured into the rice-measure it was found that it did little more than just cover the bottom, and so they had to return for more. This happened not once but many times, for it seemed impossible to fill the measure more than half full.

At length the patience of the King became exhausted. An altercation began, in the course of which the measure somehow or other got knocked off the box upon which it stood. Like a flash Tabiko stooped to pick it up, but he was not quick enough, and to their amazement the King and his son saw that in the base there was a small hole, so that almost as fast as the gold was poured in it flowed out into the box beneath.

When they realized how they had been cheated, both father and son flew into a tempestuous rage, and, after vowing that they would never again have any dealings with mortals, they summoned all the crocodiles from the realm beneath the river. Then, themselves casting off their human forms, they devoured Tabiko and all his people, including the garrulous Bangsat as he returned from his journey, so that there was not a man, woman or child in the village left alive. And from that day to this the crocodiles have nursed so bitter a resentment against the human race that they have never been seen in mortal shape again, being content to live in their domain beneath the river, and to wage unceasing warfare with the dwellers in the upper world.

The spread of his mighty wings hid the sun.

THE GERUDA BIRD

There is always something uncanny about an eclipse of the sun or the moon. In spite of what the learned astronomers say, one can never be quite sure that the great black shadow will pass away, and that the light-givers will regain their wonted brilliance. The thought that some day the sun or moon might go out for good, like snuffed candles, is disturbing enough to those who have electric light to fall back upon, but it is much more so to the wild people of Borneo, who have to depend on nature for light by which they may do their work or go about their business. To them the coming of an eclipse portends a disaster to the sun or moon, and they have to do everything in their power to avert it. Some hold that a great dragon is eating up the sun, and beat gongs and drums until they have frightened him away; some think that the sun is the moon's husband and the stars their children: an eclipse means that husband and wife are quarreling, and that one has thrown dirty vegetable water over the other, and it is only by the people on earth making a great noise that peace can be restored; others believe that the sun and moon both run along a well-defined track in the sky, each being hauled backwards and forwards by means of a great rope pulled by forty holy men. Between the two tracks is a large ditch, and into this one of the planets occasionally falls, so that the world for a time is deprived of its precious light.

The reason for either the sun or the moon deviating from the straight and narrow way is rather a roundabout story. Many hundreds of years ago an old man called . and his wife, who dwelt in a little village beside the rippling Tempassuk River near the mountain of Kinabalu, were waiting for their rice to ripen in the fields. It was a crop such as they had never known before, but, when the harvest time was drawing near, thousands of sparrows and other little birds descended upon the ripening field and began to pluck the yellow grains from the ears.

Do what they would, Usman and his wife could not keep them off nor frighten them away. They tied coloured rags to the ends of poles and set them to flutter in the field; they beat gongs and hired small boys to come and shout both night and day; they ran long strands of creepers with leaves attached above the rice, and set them in motion by pulling them all day long; they laid snares for the birds themselves. But all this was of no avail. The sparrows continued to come on in flocks, twittering and fighting to the feast. Such were their depredations that there seemed every chance of the crop being ruined utterly, and if that happened Usman knew that he and his family would surely starve, for they were very poor, and had no goods which they could barter for food with their neighbours.

The prospect became more than Usman's wife could bear, and in her exasperation she started nagging at her husband.

"Have you no wits to pit against these rascally birds?" she cried. "Must we stand here while they ruin us before our very eyes?"

Finally, in desperation, old Usman hit upon a plan. He covered his whole body with the gummy sap of a jungle tree, and sprinkled himself with grains of rice. Then, heedless of his wife's gibes, he stood quietly in the middle of the rice-field, hoping by this means to catch as many of the robbers as he could.

He succeeded beyond his hopes, for hundreds of the greedy little birds settled upon his sticky body and could not disentangle themselves, no matter how they struggled. On and on they came, until at length Usman was covered from head to foot with a mass of fluttering sparrows; more and more desperate became their efforts to escape, and Usman was just beginning to chuckle with glee at the success of his scheme when, to his horror, he found himself being lifted up into the air, so strong was the beating of those countless tiny wings.

"Ho! wife," he yelled in terror, "the birds have taken me prisoner and are carrying me away. Quick! Bring a rope and catch my feet before I am out of reach."

On hearing his cries, Usman's wife came rushing out of the house to see what was the matter, but she was too late to help her husband, who by that time was soaring above her, his legs dangling to and fro, and his hands clawing the air in vain for something that would stay his upward flight.

The fates, however, did not treat him so unkindly after all. Higher and higher the sparrows bore him until they reached a fair country on the other side of the sky where no mortal had ever set his foot before, ruled by a Sultan who had human form but magic powers. Luckily for Usman the Sultan took a fancy to him, and treated him as a guest rather than a prisoner. He lived at ease in the royal palace, eating food such as he had never known before, doing no work of any kind and sleeping upon the softest mats. To Usman it was like paradise, and he very soon forgot his home and his old wife in the village beside the rippling Tempassuk River. It was not long before he had so ingratiated himself with the royal family that he was given in marriage the Sultan's lovely daughter; the wedding was celebrated with great rejoicings, and Usman's splendid clothes presented a spectacle very different from the old coat made of tree-bark which he had worn at his first wedding-feast.

In course of time, Usman and his new wife had a daughter, who was even more beautiful than her mother, and, strange to say, when she came into the world she was found to be clutching tight in her dimpled hand a baby tortoise. As she grew up this tortoise was her constant comrade; but one day when she was about seventeen years old, it vanished from the royal garden, leaving only its tracks behind in the dusty road beyond the palace gates.

The Princess was distracted at the loss of her playmate, and, without telling anyone of her intentions, she followed the tracks along the road. Mile after mile she trudged in the blazing heat, growing more and more weary (for she was not used to walking) until at length she reached the cave of the Gergasi, an enormous ogre who had an unpleasant habit of eating human beings. He had just finished lunching off one when he spied the Princess peeping into the entrance of his cave.

"Don't be frightened, my dear," said the Gergasi, who, having had a pleasant meal, was feeling in a good temper, "but come in and sit down and tell me what you are doing along this lonely road."

"I have lost my tortoise," answered the Princess, breaking down and beginning to weep. "I have followed his tracks for miles and miles, yet I have never been able to catch him up, and now I am very tired and very hungry."

Her gathering tears made her eyes shine like stars on a moonless night, and she looked so lovely in her distress that even the Gergasi's heart was touched, and he fell violently in love with her. In a moment he became a well-meaning, good-natured old thing, and, throwing the bones he had been gnawing on to a heap of others that lay at the back of the cave, he apologised profusely for having nothing in his larder.

"The fact is," he confessed, "I have just finished the last foot. If only you had come ten minutes earlier, we might have shared it. But if you don't mind waiting a little I will go off to one of my prisons and bring back enough for a week. I shall have to hurry, for I believe my old enemy the Geruda Bird is at his little games again."

Without waiting for her reply, he seized his mighty club, that was made of elephant's hide and studded with crocodiles' teeth, and hurried out of the cave, leaving the Princess frightened out of her life. There seemed to her no prospect of getting away from the horrible cave, for she was too exhausted to walk another step, and she began to sob her heart out.

But the Gergasi had not been long gone when the Princess suddenly heard in the distance the sound of beating wings. Nearer and nearer it came, louder and louder it grew, until it seemed like the roar of a flooded torrent on a windy night. The whole cave became dark, and, looking out, the Princess saw gliding down towards her from the sky the Geruda, the biggest bird in the world, and the only enemy of whom the Gergasi stood in awe. The spread of his mighty wings hid the sun, and so vast were they that he was able to carry beneath them a thousand men whom he had rescued just in time from the Gergasi's prison. These unfortunates were clinging to his feathers for all the world like so many strap-hangers in a crowded carriage of the Underground.

The Geruda alighted gently on the road that ran below the Gergasi's cave.

"What is the matter, Princess?" asked he. "Far up in the sky, as I was taking these luckless victims of the Gergasi to their homes, I heard your weeping, and I have come to see if there is nothing I can do to help you."

"Indeed there is," replied the Princess. "I too am about to become one of the Gergasi's victims, for if he does not eat me he will want to marry me, and that will be just as bad. So I beg you to take me back to my father's palace that I may begin looking for my beloved tortoise again."

"You need have no fear for your tortoise," said the Geruda Bird, from whom nothing was hidden. "He is safe back in the palace garden again, looking everywhere for you. And if you will but catch hold of one of my feathers I will take you back to your father. But make haste, for the Gergasi will soon be home."

So the Princess caught hold of one of the Geruda Bird's feathers and soon found herself being carried through the air. Nor was it long before her deliverer gently set her down in the palace garden, and then flew away again with his other passengers.

There was much rejoicing at the return of the Princess, for her disappearance had caused everybody great anxiety, but the rejoicing was turned to dismay when a few moments later a loud bellowing was heard outside and the Gergasi, furious that the Princess had escaped him, came battering at the palace gates. Having smashed them in with his mighty club that was made from elephant's hide and studded with crocodiles' teeth, he slew the guards who tried to bar his way and strode on to the audience-chamber of Usman, who was now ruling the country as Sultan in his father-in-law's stead. The Princess had just time to pick up the tortoise (whom she had found looking for her even as the Geruda Bird had said), blacken her face and run away to hide, when the Gergasi came face to face with the Sultan.

"Where is your daughter?" he thundered. "She is to be my wife, and, while I was out collecting some meat for our wedding-feast, she left my cave and ran away."

"While she was waiting for you, good Gergasi," said the Sultan, speaking as calmly as he could but with one eye on the Gergasi's club, "the Geruda Bird came along and carried her off. It was but a few minutes ago that we heard the clamour of his wings as he passed overhead."

"As I thought! As I feared!" yelled the Gergasi. "He has robbed me of my prisoners and now he robs me of my bride!"

He gave a wild howl of rage and dashed off in pursuit, waving his club about him as he went, and vowing that he would chase his enemy to the end of all the worlds. But as he could not fly he was never able to catch the Geruda Bird. For all that, he has never abandoned the pursuit, and to this day in that fair country on the other side of the sky he chases his enemy, hoping one day to catch him as he comes to earth. In fact so busy is the Gergasi that he has no time to hunt men for food, but instead he lives on berries and roots as he rushes along. So that the Geruda Bird, who, as you have seen, is the best disposed of creatures, by keeping the Gergasi so actively employed is doing a great deal of good. Indeed, the only time that he ever does any harm is when he flies too near the ropes by which the forty holy men are hauling the sun and moon on their accustomed journey across the heavens. For then his wings are apt to become entangled, and he has such struggles to extricate himself that he causes either the sun or the moon to topple from its track into the ditch, and thus its light becomes obscured. The people of Borneo, dismayed at the failure of heaven's light, begin shouting and beating gongs and drums until they have attracted the attention of the holy men, whereupon one of the latter swarms up the rope, disentangles the Geruda Bird and pushes the planet back into its place again.

The only danger is that one of these days the holy men, who are becoming deafer every year as old gentlemen do, may fail to hear the noise that is being made on earth, for then the Geruda Bird will remain a prisoner until the end of time and the sun will never shine properly again.

The Felling of Tinagat Rock

On the eastern coast of Borneo the little township of Tawau nestles on the shores of a land-locked harbour, so vast that all the navies of the world might lie safely within its arms. To-day Tawau is a Government Station, an outpost of the Empire if ever there was one, connected with the outside world only by wireless telegraphy and by the coasting steamers which call two or three times a month. The little station is self contained: besides the Government Offices and the Court it has its own barracks, its hospital, its club, and its rest-house for the passing traveller; it is set on every side with waving coconut trees, and upon the hill where stands the bungalow of the Resident there is a shady garden with lawns looking out upon the sea, and flower-beds where roses will bloom the whole year long.

That is Tawau to-day, as delightful a home as you could find in all the East. But there were other days, days before any form of government was known in the land, before the Chinese shops existed, before ever a steamer had ruffled the waters of those tropic seas, before there was any warning light on Batu Tinagat, the rocky promontory at the entrance of the landlocked bay.

Nevertheless, Batu Tinagat was there, although not always in its present shape or under its present name. Batu Tinagat means "The Felled Rock," and this is the story of how in days of old it came to be hewn down like a forest tree.

Long ago, when Tawau was nothing but a squalid little native village, a collection of palm-leaf huts straggling along the sea-shore, there lived one Daud, a man of gigantic stature and prodigious strength. So powerful was he that he could pick up a buffalo by the horns and fling it over his shoulder without an effort, and when he paddled his canoe along by his mighty strokes, he could send it flying through the water faster than could a crew of ten.

For the most part Daud lived the life of a sea-gipsy, faring hither and thither in his boat, catching fish with his nets or striking them with a three-pronged spear as his craft glided slowly over the water at night, a flaming torch in the bows to attract the prey. Sometimes he would go in search of the round white eggs which the turtle buries in the sand, or dive for the precious mother-of-pearl shell with which those seas abound. More rarely, he would tire of the sea and live for a while in the tumble-down palm-leaf village, now and then planting a little rice or a few vegetables, enough for his bare needs and nothing else. But when he had occasion to make a clearing in the surrounding jungle for his garden, with a few blows of his great axe he could bring a lofty lord of the forest crashing to the ground, when it would have taken his fellows a day to perform the selfsame task. For this reason he was known as Daud the Strong.

One day, whilst he was sailing out at sea in his canoe, there arose a storm which blew Daud to the south and forced him to seek refuge in the mouth of a river called the Sibuku. The gale did not abate; Daud had no food and was near starvation, for the mangrove-swamps which fringed the lower reaches of the river offered little to eat but crocodiles' eggs and small brightly coloured crabs. So in desperation he began to paddle up the river, hoping to come upon a village where he would find food and shelter.

After paddling for many hours, he came to a single house upon the river-bank, surrounded by a garden in which the banana-leaves flapped to and fro; from his canoe he could see the juicy sugar-cane growing, and sweet potatoes and maize, while above, under the waving leaves of the palm-trees, hung clusters of green coconuts. Daud's spirits rose, and he gave a hail. To his joy he heard an answering shout, and down the house-ladder clambered an old man.

"Welcome, stranger," he called. "What village are you from, and whither bound?"

"I come from Tawau," answered Daud, resting upon his paddle, "but the storm has blown me from the waters that I know. For many days have I been at the mercy of wind and wave, and now I would crave food and the shelter of your roof since, although men call me Daud the Strong, I am nigh exhausted."

"Tie your boat to yonder post," said the old man, "and enter. There is none but my wife and my only daughter within, and, although we are very poor, you shall have such as my humble home can offer you."

With much relief, Daud made his boat secure and followed his host to the house. He was made welcome, and it was not long before he was eating rice and fish from a plate of fresh banana-leaves, and drinking cooling draughts of milk from a green coconut. That was good, but what seemed even better to Daud was his host's daughter, Alimah, who waited shyly upon him. She was young and slender, and her skin had the tint of an autumn leaf. Her great brown eyes allured him, and, as he watched her pattering to and fro, he longed to play with her glossy tresses of raven hair.

Day after day slipped by. The skies became fair again and the wind dropped, yet Daud could not bring himself to get in his boat and paddle away, so strong was the spell the maiden cast upon his heart. He lingered on, helping the old man with his garden and his fishing. The old people came to admire his great strength, but neither of them so much as Alimah, to whom the mighty stranger seemed the prince of all her dreams come true.

At last one evening Daud, his mind made up, sought out his host as he was mending his nets upon the river-bank.

"Father," said he, after some idle talk, "you have been my friend indeed since the day on which I came paddling up the river; both food and shelter have you given me willingly, yet before I leave for my village one boon greater than either of these would I ask of you."

The old man nodded his head.

"Speak on," he answered, though he knew well enough what Daud would say.

"It is Alimah," went on Daud. "I long to have her for my wife, and if you will but agree to let me take her back to my people I will pay you as her dowry three brass cannons and three gongs embossed with dragons."

"That would be well enough," said the old man, "but we grow old, my wife and I; would it not be better if you returned home for your cannons and your gongs, and then dwelt here with us? As you know well, that is the custom of the land."

"I have a house and garden of my own," replied Daud, "and I too must think of my own people. But if you will give me the maid you need not lose her altogether, for I myself will bring her to visit you from time to time."

"I will consult with her mother," said the old man, a little sadly, and with that he led the way into the house for the evening meal.

The next day he took Daud aside and, offering him a quid of betel-nut to chew, he said:

"It seems that the maid's dreams have been fair ones of late, O Daud, and, since her heart is set upon you and your heart upon her, my wife and I feel that we must give her to you. With your offer of three brass cannons and three gongs embossed with dragons we are content, and we will make only one condition to the marriage: that you let our daughter return to us for one night in every fourteen days."

Daud was so anxious to have Alimah for his own that he willingly consented to her father's condition. Accordingly he returned to Tawau with all the speed he could, brought back with him the brass cannons and the gongs that were to be Alimah's dowry, and handed them over to her parents. The marriage ceremony was performed by a priest who dwelt near by, and then, taking leave of the little house upon the riverbank, Daud bore his bride back to his home in Tawau village.

For some time the pair lived as happily as two squirrels in a coconut-tree. On the fourteenth day after leaving her home, Alimah remembered her promise to her parents, but Daud protested that they could not leave Tawau again so soon, and Alimah was so much in love that she let him have his way. As the twenty-eighth day approached she spoke again to Daud, but once again he overruled her, and she said no more. As the weeks went by the same thing happened every time Alimah reminded Daud of the promise, until gradually she began to languish, as the brown people will, for her own home and her own people.

The Malays have a saying, which may be translated:

> "Rain of gold in thy land, rain of stones in mine:
> Yet give me my land, nine times nine."

Every day, much as she loved her husband, Alimah began to feel more intensely how true this saying was, and, with tears in her eyes, she pleaded with Daud to take her back to the old people who, she knew, were waiting anxiously for her in their ragged house upon the banks of the Sibuku River. But the journey was a long one, even for one who could wield a paddle as mightily as Daud, and he, seeing how that the promise he had given so lightly was one that was most inconvenient to keep, still put her off.

Alimah continued to pine. Again and again she begged to be allowed to go, until finally Daud gave her nothing but a blunt refusal, hoping that in time she would forget and be content. But the call of her own people was too strong, and at last, greatly daring, she decided that, since she could not go with his permission, she would go without it and run away.

So one moonlight night, while her husband was sleeping, Alimah crept out of the house and stole off along the beach. It was not long before Daud discovered that his little bird had flown. He leapt from his mat, furious, seized the great axe which he used for felling jungle trees, and followed in pursuit. Alimah heard him coming and fled before him, like a leaf before the wind, until she reached the rocky point that is now called Tinagat. She climbed to the very summit of one of the towering crags, and from the lofty pinnacle watched her husband as he came clambering after her. Fear gripped her heart, for she knew well enough that, should Daud catch her in his present mood, he would most surely kill her with his axe, and so she began to roll down upon him some of the great stones which lay scattered upon the summit of the peak. As they went bounding past him, Daud drew back perplexed. He did not wish to lose Alimah, but neither had he any desire to have his brains dashed out by a rocky boulder. Suddenly he made up his mind, and, invoking the aid of Allah, he swung his mighty axe and started to hew down the crag. So powerful were the blows which he rained upon the rock that it was not long before it began to yield to the axe like a tree, and Alimah had only just time to leap wildly to another crag before the one on which she had first sought refuge toppled over and came crashing down.

Daud hewed down her second sanctuary as well, and even a third to which she leapt. Then, despair in her heart, but nimble as a doe, she fled again before him, springing from rock to rock until she came once more to the sandy beach, where lay a small canoe. It took her but a moment to push it out to sea, and, before Daud could overtake her, she jumped inside and began to paddle as hard as she could in the direction of her home.

In his rage, Daud rushed into the sea and tried to swim after her, but a lurking jelly-fish caught him in its stinging tentacles, and, roaring with pain, he was forced to seek the land. By the time he had found another boat Alimah was far out to sea; but he paddled furiously after her, throwing up great clouds of spray, and gaining upon her at every stroke until, at the mouth of the Sibuku River, he was close behind. Alimah shrieked when she heard the chunk of paddles drawing nearer, for she felt that the end was at hand, and that further flight was vain. But the great river, whose child she was, took compassion upon her, and caused a great wave of water to arise at its mouth and go tearing up towards its source, bearing Alimah's frail canoe upon its breast and leaving Daud far behind. On and on it swept, carrying all before it, until it came to Alimah's home; there it died down, and the rejoicing fugitive fell into her father's arms.

After the river had carried his wife out of his clutches Daud dared not follow, for he feared that her own people would come down upon him from their villages and make him prisoner, and so, in a chastened mood, he made his way back to Tawau, and took counsel with the elders of his tribe. They promised to undertake negotiations between Daud and his wife, and finally it was agreed that, if she would return to him, all would be forgiven and she would be allowed to visit her parents every fourteen days, as he had promised before he had taken her as his bride.

That is the reason why the rocky promontory, where Daud plied his axe with such a will, is called The Felled Rock, and it is the reason, too, why the bore goes rushing up the Sibuku River every fourteen days. Every native knows well when it is coming, and takes good care to keep out of its way, but when he hears it roaring past he cries:

"There is Alimah going home again."

The Spectral Huntsman

In a little Borneo village, not far distant from the sea, there once lived a man called Sampar and his wife. Sampar was a great hunter, and with his pack of seven bright-eyed, sharp-nosed dogs behind him he would range through the forests in search of game, big or small. No one in all that country-side was so quick to mark the tracks of a wild beast as he, no one could creep so silently through the thorny brake without disturbing leaf or twig. Sometimes, treading barefoot as softly as a cat, he would find a feeding stag, and setting a poisoned dart in his long blowpipe he would take a deep breath, put his lips to the mouthpiece, and then shoot out the dart at the unconscious prey with unerring aim. Sometimes his dogs would hunt a wild buffalo for many miles across the plains, up the hills, down the valleys and across the streams; then, as it began to tire, they would form themselves in a circle round it, barking and yelping until the bemazed brute knew not which way to turn, and Sampar, who, fleet of foot though he was, had been left far behind, came up and despatched it with his spear. He would set spring-traps of bamboo for the wild boar, and make pits for the shy rhinoceros whose horns were prized by the Chinese traders of the coast for making medicine. He would snare the great python as it slept gorged with a goat or a deer, and none was so daring as he in the quest of wild beeswax from the forest trees; for when night had come he would make a ladder up the side of a tree-trunk by driving in bamboo pegs, and by this means would slowly ascend a hundred feet to the branch where the swarm had settled; with a flaming torch, he would brush the nest so that thousands of bees fell stupefied to the ground, and then, heedless of the stings of those which remained, he would cram the amber comb into a basket and let it down to his waiting comrades who stood below.

One day Sampar's wife fell ill. Sampar did what he could to doctor her, bringing her herbs and healing leaves from the forest, but his efforts were of no avail. She refused all food and began to waste away.

"Is there nothing that I can do for you, dear wife?" asked Sampar in distress.

"Yes," answered his wife at last. "I have a fancy to eat the white flesh of a doe mousedeer. Go into the jungle and catch me one."

The mousedeer is a tiny animal little bigger than a hare, which abounds in the Malayan countries. A doe mousedeer would not be difficult to find, thought Sampar, and his heart was glad because his wife's behest was one which could so easily be obeyed. Straightway he called his seven dogs and strode out into the jungle, his knife at his side and his blow-pipe in his hand.

But, as luck would have it, although he hunted the whole day long he failed to bring down a doe plandok until the sun was setting, and he was far from home. In Borneo, when the sun goes down, it is as if someone had put out a giant's lamp, for there is no twilight and the whole world goes dark at once. Great hunter though Sampar was, even he did not care to wander through the mysterious forest at night, for that is the time when the evil spirits, which haunt the rocks and streams and trees, renew their powers and are to be feared, wreaking vengeance as they do upon mortals who disturb their resting places. So he decided that, instead of returning to his village that night, it would be wiser to stay where he was, and accordingly he built himself a little shelter of leaves and branches in which he might rest till dawn.

When he had finished his labours, he found that he was very hungry. The newly slain mousedeer looked extremely tempting, and he could not help feeling that it would make an excellent evening meal. For a time he banished such thoughts from his mind, remembering that he had come hunting to please his wife, and that the game was for her alone. Gradually, however, the pangs of hunger proved too much for his good resolutions, and at last, thinking that he would easily kill another mousedeer in the morning on his way home, he lighted a fire, cooked the mousedeer and had a good meal, throwing the remains to his trusty dogs.

On the following morning he started off again at dawn, but, although he hunted the whole day long, he never came upon a second mousedeer; other game he saw: roe-deer and buffaloes, honey-bears and great-tusked boars, but the mousedeer seemed to have vanished from its forest haunts. At length in despair he made his way home to the village.

"Where is the mousedeer?" demanded his wife querulously, as he climbed up the house-ladder. "Have you come back empty-handed after all this time?"

Sampar, knowing that his wife would fly into a rage if she discovered what had happened, and trusting that he would be more successful in his hunting next day, thought it wisest not to disclose the fact that he had eaten the one mousedeer he had found. So he replied:

"Two days have I hunted, wife, but never could I come upon a doe mousedeer. To-morrow at dawn I will go forth again."

So saying, he flung himself down upon his mat, tired out, and it was not long before his wide-open mouth and heavy breathing proclaimed that he was sound asleep. But his wife felt that he was hiding something from her. While he was sleeping, she crept over to his side and looked into his open mouth. There she saw the remains of the white plandok meat between his teeth.

Flying into a fury, she shook him until he opened his eyes.

"Why did you lie to me?" she cried. "While you slept I have seen between your teeth the meat of the mousedeer that you killed and ate. Are you not ashamed to treat your poor wife so?

Go forth into the jungle again! Hunt for a doe plandok and do not return until you bring it back to me!"

Sampar bowed his head. Without a word he called his dogs and set out again. But although he hunted for many days, he could never find the object of his search. Days became weeks, weeks became months, yet still he did not dare to return home without the mousedeer, for he was ashamed. Time went by, and at length, after years of fruitless wandering, he became a spirit of the jungle. The brown people learnt to fear him and called him the Spectral Huntsman. Day and night he ranged through the forest dressed in his loin-cloth and his sleeveless coat of tree-bark, as in life, and on his back was strapped the little basket for the mousedeer he could never find. His hair was long and his head was turned about, through constantly looking back to see if his quarry were behind him. He spoke to no man and he did no man harm, but the tongues of his ghostly dogs which followed him were so poisonous that, if they did but lick a mortal's footprint, he would surely die.

In the meanwhile, Sampar's wife recovered from her illness, and in course of time brought into the world a little son, who thrived and grew big and strong. As the boy grew up the village children would laugh at him and call him "the child without a father," but the older people rebuked them, for they dreaded the vengeance of the Spectral Huntsman and his dogs.

One day, when he was about twelve years old, the boy said to his mother:

"Mother, where is my father? Is he dead? Or why should he go away and let the other boys make fun of me?"

For a long time his mother would tell him nothing, but at last she answered:

"Your father is not dead, my child, but he wanders always in the jungle, hunting for a mousedeer that he can never find, and now men call him the Spectral Huntsman and fear to meet him."

Sampar's son remained thoughtful for a time, and then he said:

"Mother, I must go and find my father."

"Yes," sighed his mother, "that is your fate, my child. Go out into the jungle and search for him. You will recognise him by his pack of seven dogs, and when you meet one who walks with his head turned backwards, and his arms outstretched behind him, you will know that you have found your father."

The boy tied up some cooked rice in a banana leaf and packed it into a little basket which he strapped upon his back. He fastened his little cutting-knife about his waist, and, taking an old spear of his father's he found lying in the house, he set off bravely by himself. After he had traversed the jungle for many weary days, eking out his scanty supply of rice with roots and wild fruit, and sleeping where he could, he saw coming towards him a strange figure whose head was turned backwards, and whose arms were outstretched behind him. In one hand he carried a blow-pipe and behind him followed a pack of seven ghostly dogs. He seemed not to notice that he was being watched, and, as he passed, the boy called:

"Father!"

"Who calls me father?" cried Sampar, stopping.

"I," said the boy. "I am your son, and my mother sent me to find you."

"How can I tell that you are indeed my son?" demanded Sampar. "Have you no sign, no proof to give me?"

Then the boy told his father the whole story he had heard from his mother's lips, and showed the spear he had brought with him.

"Yes," said Sampar, examining the spear when the child had made an end of speaking, "you are indeed my son. Come, you shall be Lord of the Sea, even as I am Lord of the Jungle, and men shall fear your powers no less than they fear mine."

With that, he led his son along the dim forest tracks out on to the sunny beach. And straightway the boy, as though some new might had entered into his being, plunged into the water and was seen no more. From that day he became the chief spirit of the sea. Ha swims just below the surface of the water, a blue-flamed torch in his hand to light his way. Mortals see him seldom, but the fisher-folk fear him, for no man may look upon his face and live. In times of storm you may hear him wailing round a ship as she fights the waves, and sometimes upon inky nights he thrusts his torch above a covered reef and harassed mariners, thinking it the light of a friendly anchorage, are lured to destruction upon the rocks. The only time he ever visits the dry land is when he brings a present of fish to his father, Sampar, whom he still reveres.

As for Sampar, it is not fish he needs. Never will that troubled spirit find peace until he comes upon the mousedeer of his quest, and, great though his powers are, he seeks in vain. To this day he flits through the forests, his face turned backwards and his arms outstretched behind him, as when his son found him first. The jungle people often hear him rustling by, and when they come upon the dead body of a mousedeer they know that he has passed that way, slaying in hopes that his victim may be a doe at last. He does no one harm, and although they fear his dogs the brown men have come to be sorry for the Spectral Huntsman himself, thinking perhaps that such a punishment for one who has but failed in a domestic errand is too severe; but the women, although they may be sorry too, cannot help feeling that it is well that the jungle should hold so wholesome an example of the retribution which follows erring husbands who fail in duties set them by their wives.

The Enchanted Basket
and the Lazy Woman

The Garden of the Sun, as Borneo has been called, is not a difficult place to live in, even if one is not very fond of work. There Nature is in her most generous mood: she gives much to those who plant nothing, but to those who plant a little she gives in abundance. For food one has only to put a seed into the earth and it will grow, drenched by the life-giving rains and warmed by the kindly sun; fish teem in the rivers; game abounds in the forests, while on every side are the materials needed to build a house; there is a profusion of bamboo, whose great tubes, once split, serve as floors and walls; the jungle has timber for posts; along the river-banks crowd the graceful nipah-palms, whose leaves, when dried, take the place of tiles. Of nails there is no need, for in the forest are climbing coils of rattan which form a universal substitute, so tightly and strongly will they bind. From the bamboo can be fashioned cups, besides a hundred other household things; fresh banana-leaves make pleasant plates; fuel is at hand for the gathering; soft mats on which to sleep are easy to plait from the grasses; from grasses, too, can be woven the few clothes that are necessary, while dye to colour them can be produced from jungle roots.

It is not strange, then, that the brown people, who have lived in this pleasant land since history can remember, should not be unduly energetic, for when they have satisfied their few simple needs, which they do so easily, there seems to them no object in going further. But at least they work sometimes: although material is at hand, they have to build their houses; although crops grow easily, it is necessary to sow and reap them; water has to be carried from the stream; rice has to be husked and cooked.

There once lived on the smiling Tempassuk Plain, however, a woman called Napsi, who was so lazy that she would do none of these things. Her name was a by-word throughout the country-side. It was so much trouble for her even to walk down to the river that she seldom bathed more than once a month, and as for work—she never did any at all. It was as much as she could do to pick the bananas that grew in abundance near her house, and to save herself the bother of cooking she lived upon the charity of friends, who, although they laughed at her, were too good-natured to refuse her what she asked.

One evening, as she was sauntering home along the river-bank after one of her rare visits for a bath, she saw a nipah-palm that was growing on the other side of the stream nodding violently, although there was not a breath of wind. This was such an unheard-of occurrence that even Napsi was surprised into being interested, and she stopped to watch. Then she heard a voice, apparently coming from within the nipah, call out:

"Get into the canoe that is tied to that post, Napsi, and come over here. I have something very important to tell you."

"Can't you tell me from over there?" asked Napsi, who did not feel inclined to put herself to the trouble of paddling across the river, even though a nipah-palm was talking to her.

"No," said the nipah. "If I did, others might overhear, and what I have to say is for your private ear alone."

"What is it about?" demanded Napsi cautiously.

"I can tell you a means by which you will be able to obtain as much food as you wish, without having to work for it," replied the nipah.

On hearing this Napsi's curiosity was fully aroused, and with an effort she summoned up sufficient energy to get into the canoe and paddle across the river.

"Well, what have you got to tell me?" she said when she had got over, rather exhausted after her unwonted toil.

"If you want to get food without any trouble to yourself,"

answered the nipah-palm, "you must cut down these leaves of mine. Then take them home and make them into a large basket, such as folk use for carrying goods upon their backs. When you have made it, set it empty beside the path on a market-day. After that, leave everything to the basket; simply go back to your house and see what happens."

To the idle Napsi, even the thought of all the trouble she would have in making the basket was intolerable. However, it seemed that if what the nipah said were true she would be the gainer in the long run; so she took the leaves home, and, after much groaning and lamentation, at last made a carrying-basket from them. On the following market-day, before anyone was about, she set the basket near the path, according to the nipah's instructions, and then went back to the house.

It was not long before a prosperous village chief, called Soyot, came along and spied the basket standing beside the way.

"A brand new basket," thought he. "That is just what I want. I will take it along to the market-ground. If I find the owner I will give it back to him; if not, it will be a stroke of luck for me, and I shall have a means of bringing back my purchases."

He accordingly picked up the basket, thrust his arms through the rattan shoulder-straps and hoisted it on to his back. When he reached the market-ground he discovered a large crowd waiting for the proceedings to begin. On every side were men and women with their goods set out ready for sale or barter. There were men from the distant hills with great loads of tobacco; others with maize and unhusked rice. The people from the coast had fish to sell, and salt which they had obtained by evaporating sea-water over a fire; those from the plains had fowls and eggs, coconuts and sugar-cane, bananas and fruit of every kind. There were great round hats made of coloured rattan; there were gaudy head-cloths and handkerchiefs; there were mats and cooking-pots. At the side of the ground were some bamboo shacks where the Chinese merchants had laid out their wares in tempting array: cheap cloth, beads, looking-glasses, jewellery, and many other odds and ends to attract the unsophisticated people from up-country.

All were waiting impatiently for the signal to begin trading. The chief of the district went to the pole which stood in the centre of the ground and ran his flag up. This was the signal. In a moment the air was abuzz with conversation. On all sides shrill voices were raised in bargaining, on all sides were men and women intent on getting the best value as cheaply as they could.

The market was only held every ten days, and Soyot had many things to get. He bought a couple of coconuts and a bunch of golden bananas and placed them in the basket; then, after a prolonged haggle, a fowl, some fish and a few eggs; a roll of tobacco from the hills followed, some betel-nut for chewing purposes and a few fresh vegetables. All these purchases he packed carefully in the basket, having made a few (though not too exhaustive) inquiries as to its ownership without finding out to whom it belonged. The sun was still hot and he thought that it would be pleasant, before he started back on the journey to his own village, to squat down under a shady tree for a smoke and a few moments' conversation with some friends.

As soon as Soyot's back was turned, the basket, which was enchanted and had magic powers, quietly moved away of its own accord into the jungle that fringed the market-ground. Once hidden by the undergrowth it set off at a great speed towards Napsi's house, and did not stop until it had reached the ladder which led to her verandah. Napsi was frightened almost out of her wits when she saw the basket come running home in so extraordinary a manner, but when she looked inside her delight soon got the better of her fears. She emptied it of Soyot's purchases as fast as she could and then stored it away behind two old jars which stood in a corner of the house.

"Now to be off home, O cunning servant!"

The provisions which the basket had brought back kept Napsi in comfort until the next market-day came round, when she again placed the enchanted food-bringer beside the way. This time another man found it as he passed by; he behaved in exactly the same manner as Soyot had done, and, having taken it along with him to the market, filled it with eatables and other stores he bought; while the basket, in its turn, played the same trick upon him as it had played upon Soyot, and went running home to Napsi filled with food,

The same thing happened on the four following market-days, but on the morning on which Napsi had placed the basket beside the path for the seventh time, it so chanced that Soyot and the five other men who had been outwitted were going along to market together. When they set eyes upon the basket, each exclaimed:

"Why, there is that rascally basket that ran off with all my food!"

Then they stopped and looked at each other in surprise. They all told their various experiences, from which it appeared quite obvious that the basket was bewitched. They saw how they had been taken in and became angry, swearing that they would get even with the basket's owner. Soyot suggested a plan.

"Let us collect all the rubbish we can, my friends," he cried, "and fill up this robber of honest men. Then we can follow it home and see what manner of man is he who dares to play these pranks upon us."

The other five readily agreed to the proposal. They ran to and fro picking up all the rubbish they could find; this they crammed into the basket and finished loading it still further with stones, and by pouring liquid mud into it from a convenient buffalo-wallow.

"Now be off home, O cunning servant!" shouted Soyot with glee, giving the basket several hearty kicks, "and show your master the loot you have brought back from market this time!"

Amidst the jeers and laughter of its tormentors the basket set off towards Napsi's house, at a slow pace, for the stones were heavy. "Soyot and his friends followed at a distance, determined to discover its destination. When it reached home they saw Napsi rush out of the house, eager to see what it had brought her. Having ascertained who was the cause of their discomfiture, they returned to their villages and lost' no time in spreading abroad the whole story of the enchanted basket and its unscrupulous owner, with the result that everyone was so incensed at the manner in which Napsi had behaved that not one of those who had previously befriended her would give her so much as a handful of rice or a fish-tail.

In despair, Napsi took the basket to a market in another district where its powers were still unknown'; but either the basket had had enough harsh treatment and did not feel inclined to run the risk of more, or the charm was broken, for when she left it beside the path it never returned to her again. At length, her basket gone and her friends against her, she was forced through want of food to work for her living like other people. Nor was it long before she became a reformed character, for she not only pounded her own rice and fetched her own water, but even took to bathing every morning in the river like all her neighbours.

The Vampires came screaming through the air.

The Vampires of Tempassuk

Vampirism is a strange and very ghastly superstition, which, even to-day, is prevalent among the nations of Eastern Europe. Those who turn vampires are said usually to have been persons who have committed suicide, met sudden deaths or been notorious evil-livers, and most stories of vampires have much in common. As a rule the vampire appears at night, soon after burial, to persons with whom he was acquainted in his lifetime, and by sucking their blood nourishes the earthly body which rests within the grave. On the grave being opened the corpse, even after a lapse of years, is found fresh and rosy as in the days when it was alive; but when a stake is driven through the heart, or the heart torn out and the body burnt, nothing more is ever seen of the vampire. The place at which the vampire usually sucks the blood of its victim is the throat, and it leaves behind a blue mark like that of a mole; in one case it is recorded that a woman, who had been the victim of a vampire, was found with this blue mark, streaked with blood on the neck under the right ear, a finger long.

In these cases it is the souls of the dead who are believed to return to prey upon the living, but in the Tempassuk district of Borneo there is a race of men called Illanuns, with a sinister reputation for being able to turn themselves into evil spirits while they are still alive, and so prey upon the newly dead. They too may be called vampires for want of a better word. They are both feared and hated by their neighbours, who dare not stay in an Illanun village for a single night, and if a stranger comes seeking shelter to a house on the outskirts of the Illanun country, the inmates will go off secretly and set light to some cocks' feathers or the shavings of buffalo-horns to test him. For they believe that no vampire can withstand the smoke that rises from either of these charms, and that once it reaches his nostrils he will flee out of the house as if pursued.

The Illanuns were not always vampires, although their forebears were pirates and cut-throats from time immemorial, roving the seas in search of victims. They were devoid of any feelings of pity, and were accustomed to look upon acts of cruelty with indifference from their childhood's days, but the origin of their taste for human flesh came about in the following way.

Long ago the Illanuns had amongst them a learned man called Indog, who was their priest and teacher. Every day thirty Illanum boys went to him to be taught the Koran, but their thoughts even in those early years were turned upon war and piracy, and only one of them, who was named Amat, could be found to learn. This boy, the youngest of them all, outstripped the others in knowledge, and while he was praised daily by the holy Indog the rest were only rated for being idle pigs.

At length they became so jealous of little Amat that they determined they would have no more of him. They had been brought up to look upon bloodshed as a little thing, and one evening they gathered together in the forest and held a secret council.

"This Amat is the cause of all the insults which are heaped upon us by Indog daily," cried Sabtu, their leader. "The time has come when we must make away with him."

"Truly spoken, Sabtu," said another; "but how is it to be done?"

"The next time that Indog sends us out to collect firewood for the hearth," replied Sabtu, "let us fall upon Amat and kill him as we would kill a deer."

This proposal was hailed with shouts of acclamation by the bloodthirsty little boys, and they returned to their homes with thoughts of murder in their hearts. A few days later, Indog, according to his custom, sent them into the jungle to collect firewood. The industrious Amat was among the party, and as he was bending down to tie with a strand of creeper the bundle of sticks he had collected, Sabtu, cutting-knife in hand, crept up behind him and, leaping suddenly upon him, dealt him a slashing blow and brought him to the ground. As he fell, Sabtu's comrades rushed forward and made an end of the unfortunate boy.

Then arose a difficulty. Amat was dead, but not done with yet.

"How are we to dispose of the body?" asked Sabtu.

"Bury it here in the jungle," suggested one.

"No," said Sabtu, "for then, sooner or later, someone would surely come upon the grave."

"Burn it," said another.

"Then, sooner or later, someone would come upon the remains," declared Sabtu. "No, my brothers, we must not leave a single trace of Amat for anyone to find. There is one way only."

"What is that?" came the question in chorus from the others.

"We must cook and eat him," said Sabtu.

Their leader's scheme seemed the only one whereby all signs of their crime would be removed. Accordingly the boys made a great fire, roasted poor Amat and ate him, bones and all, so that not a vestige of his mangled body remained to tell the tale of how he had met his fate. It was the Illanun boys' first taste of human flesh, but they found it good and smacked their lips. Then they went back to the house of Indog, the whole twenty- nine of them, carrying their bundles of firewood upon their backs.

On their return, Indog, not seeing his favourite, asked at once:

"Where is Amat? You are ever late, but he is always the first back though he brings the heaviest load."

"We have not seen him, O teacher," replied Sabtu. "He left the forest with his bundle before we did, and should be here by now."

But even as the lying Sabtu finished speaking, a small clear voice they all knew to be that of Amat cried:

"Alas, holy Indog, here am I!"

On hearing these words Indog looked round in surprise, the boys in terror. But no one could be certain whence the voice of Amat came.

"Where are you, little Amat?" asked Indog.

"Here in the belly of Sabtu am I!" piped the small voice; and then like an echo came a voice from the insides of the guilty ones, and twenty-eight times were the words repeated, "Here am I!"

It did not take the holy Indog long to realize what had been his favourite's fate. In his righteous anger he took his great staff and set upon the murderers and beloboured them, calling down upon their heads curses and imprecations most terrible to hear. But so wholly evil were they become that, as each one sped through the doorway of the house, he assumed the shape of a goblin and flew up into the jungle trees.

Ever afterwards, both they and their descendants retained this strange power of turning themselves into weird ghastly forms at night, filled with the unholy desire for human flesh. Often in the evenings you can hear them screeching as they call to one another, but if their voices sound near by you may be sure that in reality they are far away, whilst if you seem to hear them calling in the distance it is certain that they are close at hand. Should you chance to hear their voices you must cry aloud:

"Ah, Spirit of Evil, I know you come from the pupils of Indog, of holy Indog!"

And at the sound of that name they will grow afraid and fly away.

But the vampires, although nowadays they seldom dare to attack the living, do not scruple to prey upon the dead. The folk who live near the villages in which the Illanuns dwell watch their dead for many days, so ravenous are these ghouls for human flesh. Every scrap of a dead body they will devour, save only the tongue. That alone they will not eat, for they know that, if they did so, they would perish as perished their kinsmen who consumed unwittingly the tongue of Ausop in years gone by.

Ausop was an old Bajau man, who dwelt with his seven sons in the Tempassuk district. In course of time he fell ill and died. His sons guarded the body until the burial had taken place in the village cemetery upon the hillside, and then on the same night, according to the custom, Lajim, the eldest son, entered upon a lonely vigil beside his father's grave.

He had not been watching long before a band of Illanun vampires, in their goblin forms, came circling and wheeling above the grave. Much as Lajim revered his father it was all he could do to stay at his post and protect the newly buried corpse, and in the morning he swore he dared not face another night. On the second night, Hassan, Ausop's second son, remained beside the grave and suffered even worse terrors than his brother, for the vampires became more daring than before, and began to scratch away the earth which covered the old man's bones.

So it went on for six nights. Every night the vampires came nearer to their prey, and every morning the son whose turn it had been to keep the lonely vigil vowed that he dared not remain beside the grave again.

On the seventh night, it was the turn of little Kassim, the youngest of Ausop's seven sons. His brothers, mindful of what they themselves had suffered, and of the fears by which they had been beset, tried to dissuade the boy from his ill-omened task.

"It were better that you should remain safely at home with us," said Lajim, "for to-night no human power can keep these ghouls from snatching our father's remains from their resting-place, and if you are so foolhardy as to rouse them to anger, it may be that you will not see the dawn."

"Then that would only be my fate," answered Kassim stoutly, "for take my turn I must. Even if I cannot save our father from his dreadful enemies at least I may be able to avenge him."

So just as the moon was rising, Kassim made his way to the hillside where the lonely graveyard stood, and hid himself behind some bushes which were growing near the newly heaped mound of earth which marked his father's grave. He had not long to wait. Soon the vampires came screaming through the air until Kassim, peering from his hiding-place, counted a score of them clustering about the grave. Their forms were other than mortal, for they had no lower limbs, and long cruel talons took the place of hands. Screeching at one another, they tore at the earth which hid the corpse of Ausop; then Kassim's heart grew sick within him as he beheld them drag forth with unholy glee the remains of his father's body, and he crouched still lower behind the leaves that sheltered him.

But the vampires were far too full of their work to notice him. Some hurried hither and thither collecting sticks and leaves, others lighted a fire and fetched water they had brought with them for their feast, whilst the rest chopped up old Ausop's body into little piece—all save the tongue, the eating of which to vampires means destruction. That they flung away into the jungle, and none noticed Kassim creep from his hiding-place to find it, as they gathered round the bubbling pot and made ready for the banquet that had been delayed so long.

As soon as their prey had been cooked to their liking they fell to, and having gorged themselves they set aside what remained in the pot for a morning meal. Then they laid themselves down to sleep, tired out by their orgy. Thereupon Kassim drew his knife from its sheath and cut his father's tongue into little pieces; bearing them in the hollows of his hands, he stole out from his hiding-place until he came to the vampires' pot, and, having dropped them in, mixed them with the other remains of the father he had loved. Then with tears streaming down his cheeks, he went back to the bushes and resumed his watch.

Before dawn was come the vampires were astir again, eager to prepare a morning meal before they should seek their homes and change back into their human forms. The fire was soon rekindled; once more the water bubbled in the pot. Each vampire seized his share of the remains and began to devour it greedily. But no sooner had he swallowed the last mouthful than he fell prostrate upon the ground. Unwittingly he had eaten of the forbidden thing which Kassim had mixed within the pot.

On seeing that his strategem had been successful, Kassim crawled out of the bushes and ran home to rouse his brothers.

"Come, my brothers, come!" he cried, triumph getting the better of his grief, "and I will show you the carcasses of our father's enemies!"

Wonderingly they followed him. As they reached the spot the first rays of the sun were lighting up the carved posts and tombstones of the lonely graveyard, and there before their father's opened grave they beheld the bodies of twenty dead Illanuns stretched upon the ground in human form.

The Cunning Mousedeer

In the good old days, when animals talked and acted much in the manner of human beings, Si Plandok, the mousedeer, was the cleverest of all creatures that went upon four legs. He was as cunning and as subtle as Brer Rabbit, and, as everyone knows, whoever tried conclusions with that sharp-witted warrior always came off second best.

The stronger his opponents, the better was Si Plandok pleased. One day, all the animals formed a kind of co-operative society for catching fish. It was agreed that the total catch should be pooled and then divided amongst the partners, each receiving a share according to his size. On the first day everything happened as had been arranged: a reach of the river was chosen where a deep pool teeming with fish flowed down towards the pebbly rapids; here the animals set the long bamboo traps into which the fish were driven by the current. In the afternoon the traps were opened, and the whole catch was deposited in one heap upon the river-bank. Then, after the animals had rested, it was divided up as had been agreed. The elephant took the largest share; the rhinoceros and the buffalo came next; the stag and the goat received medium shares; but when it came to the turn of poor Si Plandok, he, being the smallest, was only given one miserable little fish.

Si Plandok said not a word, but his active brain began to work busily, and finally he thought of a plan. The next day, after the catch had been landed upon the bank, the animals rested from their labours as before, and one by one gradually dropped off to sleep. All, that is, but Si Plandok. He remained very much awake, and going to the heap of fish he collected a quantity of their scales. Turning back to where his friends lay slumbering, he crept up and carefully plastered a layer of scales over the closed eyelids of each sleeping beast. When he had completed his handiwork without waking any of them, he suddenly started to run to and fro as if in great agitation, and shouted out at the top of his voice:

"The hunters are upon us! Fly, friends! The hunters are upon us!"

On hearing his cries, all the animals started up in alarm, and, being unable to get their eyes open, dashed off into the jungle in all directions, terrified that they would be caught or killed, while Si Plandok, smiling to himself to think how easily he had outwitted them, helped himself to as much fish as he wanted and went quietly home.

On another occasion, Si Plandok was making a good meal off some sweet potatoes that were growing on the brink of a disused well which was almost dry, and, going too near the edge, had the misfortune to lose his footing and fell in. He was much exercised in his mind as to how he was to get out again, for the sides of the well were too steep and slippery to climb.

Presently a buffalo came along, grazing peacefully as he walked; when he reached the well he looked down, and, on seeing Si Plandok, called out:

"Hullo, Si Plandok, whatever are you doing down there?"

"I am eating some earth-liver that I have found in this well," replied the cunning Si Plandok. "Have you never tasted any?"

"No," confessed the buffalo; "I didn't even know there was such a thing."

"Well, you are missing a great deal," said Si Plandok, making noises as though he were eating.

"Is it very good?" asked the buffalo doubtfully.

"It is simply delicious," answered Si Plandok, smacking his lips provokingly. "There is plenty of it. Why don't you come down and try some?"

The buffalo hated to think that he was missing a delicacy, so he jumped down and started munching lumps of earth from the side of the well.

"I don't think much of this," he grumbled; "and, good gracious me, I can't get out!"

"Don't worry about that," replied Si Plandok in a reassuring tone; "leave everything to me."

Soon afterwards a stag came by and looked over the edge. He too was induced to jump down for a morsel of earth-liver, and he was followed shortly afterwards by a goat. They both found that the earth was not to their liking at all, and when they realized that there was no prospect of getting out of the well, they began to abuse Si Plandok for the trick he had played upon them.

"There is no need to be annoyed, dear friends," said Si Plandok soothingly, "How was I to know you would not like it? Earth-liver must be an acquired taste."

"Well, you persuaded us to come down here," said the stag, "so you had better try to get us out."

"Very well," answered Si Plandok, "I have got a plan. If we all stand on each other's backs, perhaps I shall be able to look over the top and see someone who will help us."

This seemed a reasonable proposal, and the others agreed. The buffalo, being the largest, knelt down and let the stag mount on his back; the goat clambered up on to the stag and Si Plandok on top of all. As he had hoped, he was just able to jump off the goat's back into the field where the sweet potatoes were growing and ran off in great glee, leaving his victims struggling in the well.

Si Plandok was never known to lose a bet, but sometimes the methods by which he won were a little questionable. One day he met a bear in the jungle, and they sat down together for a while under the shade of a great tree. The bear began to boast how strong he was, and laughed at Si Plandok for a weakling.

All right," said Si Plandok, growing nettled. "I'll bet you that you can't kick a hole in the trunk of this tree and that I can."

The bear accepted the bet, and they agreed to meet for the

contest in seven days. As soon as the bear had gone off, Si Plandok sought out his friend the beetle and persuaded him to start boring operations on the tree. In seven days the beetle had excavated a good-sized hole, which Si Plandok proceeded to plaster up with mud and pieces of tree-bark so cleverly that no one could have detected what had been done.

When the bear arrived Si Plandok said:

"You take that side of the trunk and I will take this side, and as I am the challenger I will let you start."

The bear went round to the far side of the tree and tried his strength first. He kicked the trunk until his feet were sore, yet could make no impression whatever upon the wood. But when Si Plantok's turn came all he had to do was to kick at the carefully plastered hole. The bear was much too busy nursing his damaged toes to notice how he had been tricked, and so Si Plantok won his bet.

Si Plandok, however, did not always act selfishly, for there were occasions on which he turned his wits to good account for the benefit of other people. Once there was a poor man called Si Miskin, whose only means of obtaining a livelihood was by blowing the bellows for the village blacksmith. He was a great friend of Si Plandok's, and would always share any food he had with the little mousedeer, but he was so poor that he had not even got a knife of his own, and this was a great sorrow to him.

During the time that he worked in the blacksmith's shop, however, Si Miskin collected all the waste scraps of iron he found lying about, and stored them up in a bamboo tube. After many years had gone by, he found he had enough material stored up to make not only a knife but a splendid sword, such as chieftains wear. He determined to send it across the sea to a famous swordmaker who dwelt in Java. So he went to a trader whom he knew and said:

"All, when next you set out upon a voyage to Java, will you be kind enough to take this iron to the famous swordmaker there and ask him to make me a sword?"

"With all my heart," replied Ali, taking the bamboo tube which contained the iron from Si Miskin's hands.

A few days later Ali set off on his voyage. He placed the bamboo in the ship's hold and thought no more about it, until one rough night the tube got damaged and he saw something shining inside. Wondering what it could be, he picked up the bamboo and took it to his tiny ill-lighted cabin, where, to his astonishment, he found that it contained not scraps of iron, but gold and precious stones. Si Miskin's savings, although he knew it not, had been turned to riches owing to his patience and his simplicity of heart. The treasures came tumbling out upon Ali's mat, gleaming and flashing and making the light of the smoky lamp grow pale. Ali's heart was filled with greed at the sight. He gathered the gold and the jewels, stowed them away in a safe hiding-place, and when he returned from his voyage told Si Miskin that the pieces of iron had been eaten by worms from the bamboo until not even a fragment remained.

Si Miskin, however, did not believe that Ali was speaking the truth, and as the trader would not even pay him any compensation he prosecuted him in the local Court. But Ali was now so rich that he could afford to bribe the magistrate and judgment was given against the unlucky Si Miskin.

As he was coming away from the Court, feeling that life had nothing left to offer him, Si Miskin met Si Plandok, to whom he confided his woes.

"You must appeal to the judge from the decision of the magistrate," said Si Plandok; "for I have heard from my friend the rat, who was on board Ali's ship, that your bamboo contained in reality not scraps of iron, but gold and precious stones. You shall win the case, for I will help you."

Si Miskin agreed to do as Si Plandok advised, and promised to buy him a potato-patch of his own if they won the case.

On the day when the appeal was to be heard, Si Plandok

went to the hearth and rolled over and over in the ashes. Then in the middle of the case he rushed into the Court, which was crowded with an interested audience, crying out:

"The sea is on fire ! Look, I have been nearly burnt to death!"

The trial was forgotten and everyone, including the learned judge, ran out of the Court in his anxiety to see this unheard-of spectacle. But when they got outside and gazed towards the sea, there it was, as smiling and as blue as ever.

"You trifle with the Court's time," said the judge, frowning at Si Plandok, who was thoroughly enjoying himself. "How could the sea catch fire? It is impossible."

"Yes, indeed, O Hakim," answered Si Plandok; "but it is not more impossible for the sea to catch fire than it is for worms to eat iron away."

At this there was a murmur of assent in Court. In fact, popular opinion seemed so convinced by Si Plandok's argument, and expressed itself so strongly, that the judge, although like the magistrate he had accepted a handsome bribe from Ali, did not care to go against it. Then Si Plandok brought his friend the rat into Court. The whole story of Ali's villainy was unfolded, and the judge had no alternative but to give judgment in favour of Si Miskin and order Ali to be arrested. Thus, thanks to Si Plandok, Si Miskin recovered his fortune, and he did not forget to give his little friend the best potato-patch that money could buy in return for his invaluable help.

For many years after this Si Plandok retained his fame as the cleverest of all the animals. But even Si Plandok met his match at last, and when he was least expecting it.

He was walking along the sea-shore one evening, when he met one of the small hermit-crabs, which are so called because they make solitary abodes for themselves by burrowing in the sand.

The hermit-crab was tired of hearing Si Plandok's astuteness continually praised, and felt that it would be very pleasant to score off him.

"I suppose you consider yourself a fast runner, Si Plandok?" he said with a taunt in his voice.

"Well, I can run faster than a crab," retorted Si Plandok scornfully.

"I'm not so sure of that," said Omong, the crab. "Suppose we have a race and see? I will meet you here tomorrow evening, and we will race from this point to the river which flows into the sea seven bays away."

Si Plandok agreed, although he thought it was rather beneath his dignity to run races with a crab, and promised to appear at the appointed spot on the following evening.

Omong had no intention of testing his powers of running against the fleetness of a mousedeer, but hoped to best Si Plandok in a battle of wits. Accordingly he called together seven of his comrades and bade one of them bury himself in the sand at each of the points from which the coast-line was looped back into a little bay, instructing them to jump out of their holes when they heard Si Plandok go past.

When Si Plandok arrived for the contest, Omong showed him the starting-point and said:

"As you come to each point, call out 'Omong, are you still running?' If there is no answer you will know that you have won the race, but if you get a reply you will know that I am still keeping up with you."

Si Plandok assented. On the signal being given, he started racing along the sand as hard as he could go, without looking behind him; and so did not see the crafty Omong burying himself quickly in the sand. When he came to the first bend in the coast Si Plandok called out

"Omong, are you still running?"

"Yes," shouted the first of Omong's comrades, who had

come out of his hole as Si Plandok went past. Si Plandok pressed on, but the same thing happened at each point he reached. Every time he cried "Omong, are you still running?" he was met with an answering hail.

Utterly unable to account for the way in which Omong was keeping up with him, he redoubled his efforts, putting forth every ounce of strength, for he felt that, after all his victories, it would be a shameful thing to be beaten by so humble an adversary. On and on he ran, but as he passed the sixth point and heard the answering call his strength and courage gave way. He could bear no more and he crumpled up exhausted upon the sand. The renowned Si Plandok was beaten at last, and from that day to this the hermit-crab is famous as the only creature which has ever succeeded in getting the better of the cunning mousedeer.

THE ORANG'S BRIDE

Long ago, on one of the little coast villages of North Borneo, lived Fatima, a child of the sea-gipsies. Her great round eyes were as brown as chestnuts, and she was very young. Her ancestors had been pirates and warriors who roved the seas in their war-canoes, searching for slaves and plunder. Her husband, Buna, was of the same breed; he was a Bajau, bright-eyed, a lover of gay clothes, dashing and reckless, with a right arm well trained to wield the native sword.

Fatima and her husband were as happy as the sunny days of that jungle land, in their crazy little palm-leaf house which formed part of the pirate settlement. Their lives were as unruffled as a lake at sunset until the day came for Buna to go off on one of the long piratical cruises and Fatima had to be left behind.

"Can I not come with you and share your dangers, my husband?" once she begged.

"Surely Fatima would be afraid?" he asked half teasingly.

"Afraid, perhaps," she answered, " but at least I should be with you. Left here alone without your protection I fear still more."

"Then you must send away your fears, sweet Fatima," said Buna, fastening on his coat of mail over his scarlet tunic, "for the village is well protected by those of us who are left behind. No human enemy would dare attack you here, but beware that you go not into the jungle alone, for you are so beautiful that the orang-utan, the man of the woods who dwells in the lofty forest trees, might fall in love with you and carry you away."

But Fatima only laughed at his warning and tossed her head. *"Cheh,"* said she, "woman I may be and afraid of wandering head-hunters, but I should be a coward indeed were I to be scared of monkeys."

Buna said no more, but went off in his war-boat that held a hundred warriors. The great craft had a carved figure-head and was broad of beam; she was equipped with lateen sails and with a double tier of oars. At first the oars were manned by the pirates themselves, for they took no crew in order that they might have more room for slaves whom, once captured, they set to work in chains, releasing the fighting men for battle. Sometimes they would attack openly a peaceful trading boat, overhauling her and firing missiles from their brass cannons when they had come to close quarters, then leaping on board, yelling their war-cries and brandishing their swords, athirst for blood and booty. Sometimes they would use guile and send their men out in small canoes, disguised as harmless fishermen; these warriors, coming alongside a friendly boat, would suddenly fall upon the unsuspecting occupants and make them prisoners, or, if they fled, pursue them and yank them into the water by means of long poles shod with barbed heads of iron. Nor did they confine their activities to the sea, for they would penetrate the rivers and make a sudden onslaught on a village of aborigines as it lay sleepy in the sunshine; the men they would kill or capture, the women and children they would carry off to sell as slaves; they would ravage the fields, loot the rice and brass and other valuables that were stored within the houses, and then set fire to the stricken village, shouting with glee as they watched the flames rise heaven-high.

This was the life that Buna had always known and always loved. But while he was plundering upon the high seas and capturing the wives of peaceful traders, he little knew that the wife of the chestnut eyes, whom he loved so well, was in a danger even more terrible than they, and that his home was being robbed just as he himself was robbing the homes of others.

One evening, a few weeks after Buna had left her, Fatima, rather lonely and disconsolate, finished pounding her rice and, taking a long bamboo, set off to fetch water from the stream behind the village. She was alone, for, as there were no head-hunters abroad, she disregarded her husband's warning and laughed at the fears of the other women, who never dared to go for water save in parties of three or four.

Just as she had passed a clump of fruit trees that clustered beside the narrow path, she heard an unaccustomed rustling among the leaves. Then came a stealthy movement behind her. As she turned her head, suddenly afraid, she felt two strong arms wind about her, two great long arms covered with red-brown hair; their grip was of iron, and, with a wild fluttering of her heart, she found herself looking into the baleful eyes of the dreaded orang-utan, the ape-like man of the woods. Screaming, she tried to tear away the clutch of his fantastic hands; but as well might she have tried to pluck away a python's coils as to move those clinging fingers from her hair. Nor was there anyone at hand to hear her cries, and no one came.

Without hurry, without haste, yet persistent and relentless as a fate, the orang-utan half dragged, half carried the frightened girl through the dense undergrowth; the thorns and creepers cut her face and tore her soft skin, and so tight was the embrace in which her captor held her that she could scarcely breathe. At last, everything went black before her eyes, and she knew no more.

When Fatima came back to the world again, she found herself high up on the branch of a lofty durian tree in the virgin forest. The durian is the fruit most loved by the natives of Malaya; it is as large as a coconut, its skin is covered with great spikes, and, although its smell is weird and almost disgusting, the creamy seeds within are—so some think—food fit indeed for gods. The tree's mighty grey-blue trunk rose a hundred feet from the ground without a branch, straight and smooth as a column, yet somehow the orang had brought his fainting captive to its leafy heights. It was a prison from which there was no escape.

As Fatima opened her eyes, the orang-utan was busy making a nest, snapping the branches with his hands as though they were but twigs and bending them inwards to a common centre. In a little while his work was done, and Fatima found herself dragged towards it, and placed quite gently upon the twisted boughs. Then her captor left her, making his way slowly and deliberately among the branches of the jungle trees, never trusting his weight to one until he had tried its strength. For a few moments she listened to his rustling course; then all was still. With beating heart she tried to find some means by which she might reach the ground, but the durian-trunk was too big and straight to climb, even for a native of the jungle, and, although the orang could make his way for miles by swinging from tree to tree, there was no bough within her reach to which she dared trust herself, and she feared a fall to the dizzy depths below.

Presently the rustling of the leaves began again and the orang was back, bringing her fruit to eat. As the days went by he was almost tender, and did her no harm. Every morning he would fetch food for her, and give her water to drink from the hollows of the leaves. Weeks passed, and still she lived on in the orang's nest; she longed for death, yet dared not take her life against the faith of Islam; she prayed that Buna would come to look for her and find her prison, or that some of the hill-men would pass by and shoot the orang with a poisoned dart from one of the long blowpipes they used so well.

But although Buna, back from his piratical cruise, and almost distracted by his loss, scoured the forests for his missing wife, he never found the orang's nest, which was far from the haunts of men, and so well covered by the leafy forest that, even had Buna chanced that way, it would have been hidden from his eyes. So help from the outside world never came to the lonely prisoner, and in course of time she bore the jungle man a little son. The baby's head and arms were like his father's, and covered with long red hair, but his legs and feet were those of a human being. Fatima's heart grew even heavier than before at this shame she had brought into the world, and she longed more than ever to be free.

At last she hit upon a plan. One morning, as the orang was setting off in search of food, she told him (for after all those months she could make him understand) that she had a desire for a draught of coconut milk. As he swung off into the forest he gave a grunt of assent, and when he returned he brought with him two green coconuts which he had looted from the trees of a village near the coast. Every day she asked for more, and every day, little dreaming (for all his cunning) of her plan, he brought them, even though he sometimes risked his life, for the villagers, furious at the loss of their nuts, lay in wait for him, shooting at him with their blowpipes and flinging spears.

Fatima, however, recked little of the dangers he ran, although, if her bid for freedom were to succeed, she did not want him to be killed, for he was necessary to her plans. She urged him to defy the villagers, and every morning, when he had left her, she set to work tearing at the tough coconut husk with her teeth and fingers. From the green husks she pulled strips of the strong brown fibre and wove them deftly into rope, hiding her work amongst the leaves when she expected the orang to return.

It was not for many weary weeks that her patient task was done, but there came at last a day when she found that the rope was long enough to reach the ground. With trembling fingers she tied one end firmly to a branch and let the other fall; then, leaving her baby in the orang's nest, she let herself slip slowly to the ground.

Despite her fears the rope held, and once safely upon the dear earth again she turned her face towards the sea. But, because she had not walked for so many months, her course was slow, and in the meantime her jungle husband, a green coconut in his hand, arrived back, only to find the nest empty save for his baby son. The dangling rope of coconut fibre told him plainly enough how his bride had outwitted him, and he set off in pursuit without delay.

So it was that, just as she saw the blue sea dancing behind the lattice of the jungle, Fatima heard in the distance an uproar among the branches, and the voice of the orang-utan raised in rage. *"Kogyu, kogyu,"* came his cry; half howl, half cough it seemed, and the sound lent wings to her weary feet. Nearer and nearer came the orang overhead, his long arms outstretched to their fullest length as he swung rapidly from tree to tree, but before he could reach the ground and seize her in his loathed embrace, Fatima burst her way through the fringe of jungle that separated her from the coral beach. The fates were kind to her, for there was a little fishing-boat in the act of putting out to sea, and wading out waist deep she scrambled in, leaving the orang-utan howling upon the shore.

Only the sea had saved her, for the baffled orang could not even swim a river and dared not try to follow. So he went back to his leafy nest again, in his fury breaking off great branches of the trees as he went and hurling them to earth. Once he had gained his nest he seized his baby son, and, with fresh howls of rage, bore him through the tree-tops to the shore. From afar, Fatima saw him tear the strange mite in twain, flinging all of him that was human into the sea after his mother, and all that was ape back into the forest whence he came.

The fishermen carried Fatima safely back to Buna, and the man of the woods never caught his one-time bride again. But whenever they hear an orang-utan making his strange guttural cry aloft in the jungle trees, the brown people exclaim:

"There is Kogyu looking for his lost Fatima, to take her back to his leafy home."

The Rajah watched her afar.

The Princess from under the Lake

The brown people of Borneo have a strange veneration for certain jars, which they worship with great ceremony and elaborate ritual. These sacred jars are of greenish-brown porcelain, and stand about four feet high; in appearance they are not unlike those associated with the robbers in the tale of Ali Baba, and they are the most valued possessions the natives have. They are tended by priestesses, usually widowed crones of great age, who conduct the rites when the ceremonies of the jars are held.

The time for the jar festival is made known to one of the priestesses by an old man appearing to her in a dream and asking for food. The jar is then set out in the house with a number of satellites round it; it is hung with costly cloth-of-gold and decked with valuable bead necklaces. The whole village is invited to attend, and every night for six nights there is feasting and dancing. On the sixth night the priestesses come forth. Seating themselves on the floor of the house they chant aloud in a strange jargon which no one but the initiated can understand; then they administer food and drink to the sacred jar—a few grains of rice and a little coconut wine, This done, the onlookers form a procession and march round the house, led by the priestesses, who tap the posts of the house with their small brass ceremonial knives in order to drive out any evil spirits which may have taken up a temporary abode within. The keepers of the jar then retire, and the feast is kept up, long and loud, far into the night.

The sacred jars are of great antiquity. In fact, so old are they that no man knows their maker, and their origin is lost in the mists of myth. Some are believed to be the handiwork of dragons; some dropped like thunderbolts from heaven; some were born miraculously in the depths of the virgin forest and were found by certain privileged persons, when others saw nothing before them but a tangle of undergrowth and weeds. There is one account of their origin, however, stranger than all of these, and that is the story of Rajah Nerudin and the White Princess.

Rajah Nerudin lived in a palm-leaf palace built over the unruffled waters of a great lake in Sarawak. He was young and handsome; he had inherited great possessions, and ruled over a prosperous and contented people, most of whom were fishermen; but, unlike most of his fellow rulers, he had no queen to share his throne.

One evening, he was walking beside the water's edge with a few of his courtiers, when he saw a small canoe coming home from the day's fishing, the paddlers of which, instead of singing their droning songs as was their wont, were chattering and gesticulating together as if perturbed by some strange event. Wondering what could be the cause of the excitement among his usually impassive subjects, he bade one of his attendants hail the boat, and as she came to the shore and ran aground he summoned the helmsman to his presence.

"Why is it, Abdullah," he asked, "that you and your comrades are in such a flutter to-night, like hens who have seen a hawk? Can it be that some monster has risen from the deep and set upon your boat!"

"Master," replied Abdullah, bowing low, "no monster has attacked us. But an hour ago our eyes beheld a stranger sight than they have ever seen before."

"Tell me," commanded the Rajah, becoming interested.

"As we went to examine the bamboo cage where we trap our fish," said Abdullah, his voice still trembling with excitement, "suddenly there arose out of the water the body of a woman. Whether she was mortal or not I cannot say. Her skin was not like ours, but as fair as pearl-shell; her lips were as red as the flower of the hibiscus, and her hair was as golden as the honeycomb, whilst her eyes, instead of being brown like those of our own women, were as deeply blue as the lake under a cloudless sky. She seemed more beautiful than any of our race. For a moment she gazed at us. Then, without a word, she vanished beneath the surface of the water and was seen no more. We knew not whether the meeting might portend good or evil, and we came swiftly home."

Rajah Nerudin stood silent for a moment, deep in thought. Then he said:

"If this maiden is as lovely as you say, it seems that there is no need to fear that her designs are evil. But watch well, Abdullah, and bring me word should you chance to see her face again."

The Rajah walked back to the palace pondering deeply on the story of the maiden from under the lake. It did not occur to him to doubt Abdullah's words, for he, like all his people, knew well that there were in the world beings other than mortals, a sight of whom was occasionally granted to some. But the more he thought of the white maiden, the more desirable did she become, and he began to long to see her for himself; so much so that, on his return, he sent for an aged woman who was renowned above all others for her mystic powers.

The old dame came hobbling into the royal audience chamber, her staff tapping on the floor. She was bent nearly double, but her eyes were bright, even though time had left her face creased in a thousand wrinkles, as an outgoing tide sometimes leaves the face of a sandy beach. The Rajah told her of the fisherman's strange meeting with the white maiden, just as he had heard it from Abdullah's lips.

"You are wise, mother," he ended. "You know all the tales and the traditions of the lake. Tell me, then, have you ever heard aught of this strange being before?"

"O Maharajah," quavered the old crone through her toothless gums, "this must indeed be no other than the Princess who rules over the people beneath the lake. The old stories say that these folk have human shape and form even as ourselves, but, instead of living over the lake as we do, they have the power to dwell beneath its water. Over them there rules this White Princess, who never dies, but she and her subjects harm none of us, and so seldom do they ever come to the surface of the lake that the tales about them are forgotten, and it is only I, who am so old, that can remember."

"Is there no means by which we can find the White Princess again?" asked the Rajah eagerly.

"I know of none," replied the crone. "Only, O Maharajah, if you desire to see her, call to her yourself, and perhaps she will come again or give some sign."

The old woman hobbled away and left the Rajah to his thoughts. As the days went by, so far from forgetting the White Princess, he became more and more in love with her; he longed to see her, to hold her in his arms, to make her his queen,

Often in the evenings, when all was still, he would take a canoe and paddle far out into the lake, hoping that he might catch a glimpse of her.

"White Princess," he would cry, "show me your face, for I long to see you. Come to me, for I ache to have you for my own."

But there was no sound save the faint splash of a fish, as it leapt from the water and fell back again, or the chunking of paddles in the distance as a fishing-boat went home.

Sometimes he would wander by the banks of the lake as the moon was rising, straining his eyes across the water for a sight of her whom he had come to love so much.

"White Princess," he would cry again, "rise from your palace beneath the lake. If you will but come to me you shall be my queen, and rule over my people as well as yours."

But his only answer was the chirping of a cricket in the jungle, and the music of a deep-toned gong as it floated across the silent water.

For many weeks the love-sick Rajah languished, pining for the White Princess who gave no sign. At last, one day, when he had abandoned himself to despair, the wrinkled crone came to the palace and craved audience. She was led hobbling to the presence of the Rajah, and, after speaking of other subjects for a while, as is the custom of the brown people, she said:

"O Maharajah, last night tidings came to me from the dwellers beneath the lake."

At her words, the light, so long dim, kindled again in Nerudin's eyes, and hope stirred his heart once more as the first breath of a coming breeze stirs a drooping sail.

"Speak quickly, mother," he implored, "What have you to tell me?"

"Last night in a dream," continued the old woman, "there came a message. The White Princess, whom you are seeking, has heard your passionate entreaties, and her heart is touched. Therefore your prayers will be granted, and you will see her face. On the night of the full moon be ready and prepare a feast, for on that night she will come with all her people. Let every door and every window in the palace be opened wide. Let none stay her coming, but let none stay her going either, for before the dawn she must return to her realm beneath the lake. Nor may you address a single word to her or to her subjects, for that is forbidden too, and woe betide you if you disobey."

The Rajah was overjoyed at the old woman's words. So elated was he at the thought that he would soon behold the being whom he desired more than anything in the world, that he troubled little about the conditions which were imposed. He gave orders for a feast to be prepared on the night of the full moon; he commanded that every door and window of the palace should be opened wide, and that, on pain of death, no one should stay either the coming or the going of the White Princess and of her people.

On the night appointed the feast was held. The palace was gaily decorated with palm-leaves and strips of coloured cloth and lighted by a thousand tiny lamps, while round the walls were ranged brass pots and ornaments, which had been handed down from generation to generation of the royal line. The great gongs which are indispensable at every festival of the brown people boomed out with shivering notes across the water, and the dancing girls swayed to and fro, their voices raised in a chanting song. The Rajah's ministers and courtiers thronged the halls in all the splendour of their jewelled turbans and cloth-of-gold. On one side of the royal audience-chamber had been placed a divan covered with silken cushions and costly mats in readiness for the people of the lake; dishes of sweetmeats, and trays containing betel-nut and tobacco had been set out.

But the night wore on and still there was no sign of the White Princess. The Rajah's spirits sank, and he feared that the tidings of the old woman's dream would not be fulfilled. Then, just as he was beginning to despair, suddenly the lake-folk came thronging through the palace. Through every door and window they came, and last of all the White Princess, escorted by her attendants. Nerudin's heart beat wildly as he saw that, even as Abdullah had said, her skin was as fair as pearl-shell, her lips as red as the flower of the hibiscus, and her hair as golden as the honeycomb, whilst her eyes were as deeply blue as the lake under a cloudless sky. She was more beautiful than any of his race; she was all he had dreamed she was.

Without giving him a glance, without looking to the right hand or to the left, she made her way to the place that had been prepared for her and seated herself, while her people gathered near her, ate their fill, smoked the tobacco and chewed the betel-nut as though they were human beings. But the Princess spoke never a word, and the Rajah watched her from afar.

And as he gazed upon the face he had longed to see for so many weary weeks, he began to realize how hard to keep were the conditions of the dream. To see her sitting in his own palace, calm and beautiful, and to be able to breathe never a word of his love into her ear seemed more than he could bear; he felt that if she must leave him without a word his heart would break. For a while he tried to stay his passion, but as well might he have tried to stay the waters of a flooded stream. At last he made a resolve. He would risk all in the hope of gaining all. He called his captains to him.

"The orders that were given to you are set aside," he said, speaking in an undertone. "Wait until the gongs cease their music, and then let every door and window in the palace be closed and barred. Make all the lake-folk prisoners save the Princess, but harm them not. The rest leave to me."

The captains departed, although not without misgivings of their own, to have the Rajah's orders carried out. Suddenly, at a gesture from the Rajah, the gong-beaters ceased their music, and, on the given signal, every door and window of the palace was closed as if by a magic hand. But before any of his subjects had time to lay hands upon the lake-folk, the Rajah, with his arms outstretched, advanced to where the White Princess was seated.

"Beloved," he cried, "at last I may hold you in my arms, at last…"

But his passionate appeal was never finished, for while the words were trembling upon his lips, the White Princess and all her people, in spite of the barred windows and the bolted doors, vanished from the palace as bubbles vanish from the surface of a stream. At the same instant a great wind came tearing and screaming from the hills, and the waters of the lake rose in tumultuous anger and lashed against the palace steps.

Then, as suddenly as it came, the storm died away, leaving a deathly stillness in the royal halls. Gongs and laughing voices were silent; the chant of the dancing girls was heard no more. For where, but a moment before, had been the courtiers and the captains and the swaying maidens, there was nothing but row upon row of jars. Some were standing, some were fallen, some were leaning one against the other, while in the centre of the chamber, near the cushions upon which the White Princess had lately rested, and where Rajah Nerudin had lately stood, was one jar larger than the rest, peerless and without a flaw.

The Magic Beanstalk

Before the beginning of the world, if one may believe the Dusuns of Borneo, there was nothing but a vast expanse of sky and water, and no earth of any kind. Then there fell from the sky a gigantic rock, half of which, deep as the sea was, protruded bleakly above the surface. In the top of this rock was an opening which led to a gloomy cavern, whence emerged Kinaringan and Munsummundok, the two beings who were to become the deities of the Dusun people.

For some time the pair sat together upon the rock. Then Kinaringan decided that he would trust himself to the water, and found that he could walk upon it. He called his wife, Munsummundok, and they journeyed across the waste of sea until they reached the abode of an evil spirit named Bisagit, who lived far away on the edge of the region where sky meets sea. Bisagit had been cleverer than Kinaringan, for he had somehow or other contrived to make land for himself, and Kinaringan thought that it would be an excellent plan to make some too, especially as he had conceived the idea of creating human beings, but had nowhere to put them once they were alive. So he said to Bisagit:

"Will you give me some of your earth, Dweller on the Edge of Nowhere? I wish to make some human beings, and I have no land upon which they can live."

"Very well," replied Bisagit, "but you can only have it in return for permission to take a toll of half your men every forty years."

"How would you take them?" asked Kinaringan doubtfully, for he did not much appreciate the idea of the spirit of evil being able to make havoc among the beings he intended to create.

"I shall claim them by visiting your earth as the scourge of small-pox," said Bisagit evilly, "and carry them off in that manner."

Kinaringan was no little concerned by Bisagit's answer, but as he could not make human beings unless he had land to put them on, and as he could not get the land on any other terms, he finally agreed to the conditions. Without further ado Bisagit gave him some earth, and Kinaringan and Munsummundok took it back over the waters to their rock. Then they set about breaking up the rock and mixing Bisagit's earth with it; the substance so made spread in a miraculous manner and became the world; the remains of the rock becoming the lofty mountain of Kinabalu, which to-day is the resting-place of departed Dusun souls.

Having accomplished the first part of his design, by which time Munsummundok had borne him a son and daughter, Kinaringan was free to turn his attention to peopling the world he had made with human beings. First of all he hewed from stone two images of mortal shape in male and female form, but so cold and unresponsive was his material that he could not quicken his images with life. He tried again with wood, but met with no better result. Then he bethought him of clay, and once more he fashioned two human forms; this time, the clay being soft and easy to mould, he was able to breathe life into his images and they became human beings, the ancestors of the race. That they might have light, Kinaringan made the sun, and Munsummundok the moon and the stars. And, as they had been made from the earth, Kinaringan ordained that, when they died, they should be buried in the element whence they came.

First of all the man and the woman lived upon leaves and roots, but as time went on they began to clamour for something more pleasant to the taste. For a while Kinaringan was perplexed, and finally, seeing no other way, he decided to sacrifice his daughter, so that his people might have food to eat. So the girl child was killed and cut up into pieces, which were given to the man and the woman to plant in the ground. From the child's head sprang the coconut, which, in hot countries, is the greatest boon man has; from the arms came the juicy sugar-cane, from the fingers bananas, from the legs sweet potatoes, and from the feet maize. But as yet there was no rice, which today is the chief food of the brown people.

At this time Kinaringan also made some of the lower animals—the dog, the goat, the bull, and also the fowl—by the same methods he had employed for making his man and woman, but he put on the earth no pests such as monkeys, which destroyed foodstuffs, nor snakes and scorpions which endangered human life.

After this, Kinaringan rested awhile from his labours, and, feeling that he had done his best to make the earth a pleasant place for his people to dwell in, he departed with Munsummundok to a dwelling in the sky, which they still inhabit. But the man and the woman were still not satisfied.

One day Kinaringan looked down on the earth and saw the woman weeping bitterly.

"Why do you grieve?" he asked. "Have I not given you a fair country in which to dwell? Have I not given you light by which to see? Have I not given you animals for your companions, and sacrificed my daughter that you may have pleasant things to eat?"

"Nevertheless, O Kinaringan," answered the woman, "we lack something still."

"What more can you desire?" demanded Kinaringan.

"We desire to have children," said the woman, "even as you and Munsummundok."

Now Kinaringan's son, who was named Torob, was the bane of his father's life. He was the soul of mischief, and was ever plotting some fresh malicious prank. Therefore Kinaringan was not at all sure whether the gift of children would be an unmixed blessing to his mortals, but notwithstanding this he granted them their wish, and in time gave them a family of seven boys and seven girls. When these children had grown up the seven brothers married the seven sisters, and each pair in turn had a family of seven boys and seven girls as well.

Kinaringan, although he realized that it was inevitable at first, did not like the idea of brother marrying sister, and, as he wanted to get the whole world populated, not merely one corner of it, he collected all the grandchildren of the original couple and put them into seven baskets, and in no one basket were there brothers and sisters, but only cousins. He hung these baskets up on a long pole and sent down a tempestuous wind roaring and howling from the sky, with the result that the baskets, each carrying fourteen cousins, were blown to various corners of the earth. One fell in the land that is now the white man's, one in China, one in Japan, one in Africa, one in India, another in Singapore, and the seventh in Borneo. All the occupants of the baskets landed safe and sound, and straightway set about founding races of their own.

The Borneo family flourished and multiplied until, after forty years, Bisagit, in the shape of the spirit of Small Pox, not unmindful of the bargain he had made with Kinaringan, swept through the land and carried off half their number. After this they were much distressed, for during the sickness no one had tended the fields and consequently there was little food. One day a survivor called Kabong was walking through the forest, looking for roots, when he saw a large bean lying upon the ground. He picked it up and took it home, but it did not occur to him to plant it, and he gave it to one of his children to play with. The child dropped the bean in the depleted garden and forgot all about it, but when Kabong woke up next morning he found, to his amazement, that it had sent forth a shoot which already reached above his head. The following morning it was taller than the highest tree in the jungle, and on the third day he could no longer see the top, for it vanished in the sky.

Kabong was as inquisitive as he was reckless, and he made up his mind to climb the magic beanstalk and pay a visit to the

Climbing far above the clouds.

sky. He was well used to climbing coconut trees and so he needed little practice, but the beanstalk was so tall that it took him several hours to reach the top. But at last, climbing far above the clouds, he found himself in a fair country.

"This must be the land in which Kinaringan dwells," said Kabong to himself. "That is well, for now I can ask him to send some more food to the earth for his starving people."

So he marched along, and had not gone far when he met Torob, Kinaringan's son.

"What are you doing here?" demanded Torob.

"I climbed up by the magic beanstalk," replied Kabong, "and I am on my way to see Kinaringan, that I may beg him to send more food to the earth, for while Bisagit was scouring the land all our gardens were left unplanted and we have nothing to eat."

"I will save you the trouble, good Kabong," quoth Torob, "Here is the best food in the world."

With that he handed Kabong a basket of unhusked rice, but without telling him how to prepare it for food, or giving him any directions as to how to plant it, for he thought it would be a splendid chance to play an amusing trick upon the human beings, whom he cordially detested. Kabong took the rice gratefully and thanked Torob for the gift. Then, wishing to waste no time in giving some relief to his starving people, he climbed down the bean-stalk and returned home.

Everyone was delighted to hear that he had brought back a new kind of food from the country of Kinaringan himself; all dipped their hands greedily into the basket and crammed the unhusked rice into their mouths, but in that state it was so unpalatable that they had to spit it out, and remained as hungry as they had been before.

Kabong cursed Torob very heartily for the trick he had played on them and flung the basket upon the ground. There it lay forgotten, but the dogs started worrying it until a hole was made in it, and the rice was scattered upon the ground, where it germinated and began to grow. At first the people thought it was nothing but a weed, and took no further notice of it, but when it grew into ear and began to ripen they realized that it was something more.

Kabong decided that the best course would be to take it up to Kinaringan and ask his advice. Accordingly he climbed up the beanstalk again, and this time found Kinaringan himself, who was very angry at the trick Torob had played, and at once showed Kabong how to remove the husk by pounding the rice with a long pole in a wooden mortar.

Kabong, delighted, hurried down the beanstalk and set the women pounding the rice. When it was all husked, however, they were no better off, because Kinaringan had omitted to show Kabong how it should be cooked, and fire was then an unknown element. In despair, Kabong put some of the rice in a pot filled with water, hoping that, if he let it soak it might become softer and more fit to eat. Then, calling his dog, he went off into the jungle to look for roots with which to stay the pangs of hunger.

As he was walking along he passed a large clump of bamboo that was swaying in the breeze. Suddenly he noticed smoke—something that he had never seen before—coming from two great stems which were being rubbed violently together by the action of the wind. Spellbound, he stood watching, when all at once the bamboo burst into flames. Soon the whole clump was blazing. Kabong's dog was no less startled than his master, and, barking furiously, he seized a burning brand in his jaws and made off home as fast as he could run. Still holding it, he scrambled up the house-ladder and then, as it became too hot for him and began to singe his whiskers, he dropped it on the floor. The building was only made of dried palm-leaves, and in a moment the whole place was ablaze, while the distracted Kabong looked on aghast.

The fire only lasted a few minutes, for it does not take long to burn a palm-leaf house, and the whole place was reduced to a heap of smouldering ashes. Kabong began to poke about in them to see if he could save any of his few valuables, when he came upon the pot of rice which had been soaking, and found to his surprise that it was now white and soft. He quickly called his people, and they fell upon the new food greedily, but did not forget to throw a ball of it to the dog which had been the cause of their solving the mystery of the uneatable rice.

For a while, all went well with Kabong and his people. They had food in plenty; they started to multiply again, No sooner had they recovered from their former afflictions, however, than there began a period of torrential rains, which for weeks did not cease either by day or night. A vast volume of water came pouring down from the hills; the rivers became flooded and overflowed their banks; gardens were ruined; houses disappeared; the flood rose above the level of the forests, and finally the whole country became submerged beneath one limitless expanse of water, leaving only the magic beanstalk towering to the sky.

Many of Kabong's people were drowned, but those who survived built a large raft of bamboo on to which they crowded, taking as much of their livestock with them as they could. They roofed the raft with grass and palm-leaves, thereby gaining some protection from the streaming rain, and floated aimlessly upon the flood. One morning they were aroused by the cackling of a hen; they awoke to find that she had laid an egg on the summit of a high hill which was protruding above the level of the water, and realized with joy that the flood was beginning to subside. After many days the earth became dry once more, but the precious rice, the secret of which they had found after so much trouble, had been washed down to the flat land near the sea many miles away, where it became known as wet rice, and to this day will only grow when planted in water. Once more they were in despair.

All but Kabong. He, nothing daunted, for the third time climbed up the beanstalk, which was still standing, and, when he had reached the land of Kinaringan, again met Torob, whom he persuaded to give him another basket full of rice. Before he departed for his own country, thinking that he might as well get all he could while he was there, he asked Torob if he had anything else to give away.

"If I can help you, I will do so with all my heart," answered the cunning Torob, in whose mind the memory of the way he had been bested eventually over the rice still rankled. "Here is the key of a secret box belonging to my father. If you care to, you are welcome to open it and see what it contains."

"Very well," said Kabong eagerly. "Give me the key and let us see what we can find."

Torob handed over the key, and Kabong, having unlocked the box, lifted the lid. As he did so, out tumbled a number of monkeys, scorpions, snakes, centipedes, mosquitoes, and every other living thing that is to-day a plague to man or a menace to his crops.

On seeing this Torob pretended to be very much upset.

"On his return, my father will be furious at what you have done," he cried. "You must waste no time, but take these creatures back with you to the earth, and then he may never know they have escaped."

"Why not put them back into the box?" suggested Kabong sensibly.

But when he tried he found that the lid of the box was shut fast (the wily Torob had seen to that) and could not be opened even with the key; so, feeling that there was no help for it, he caught the creatures in a bag which Torob obligingly lent him and took them down the beanstalk, hoping to be able to fling the bag into a river and drown the occupants as soon as he reached the ground. But the monkeys and snakes struggled so violently that, before he could reach the bottom, the bag fell out of his hands, and all the creatures escaped into the jungle, where they lived and multiplied.

When Kinaringan discovered what Torob had done, he was very angry, and, weary of the continual pranks of his mischievous son, he picked him up by one leg and flung him down to the earth. There he remained, playing every imaginable trick he could upon mortals, until Kinaringan listened to their entreaties and took him back again. But as Kabong had not been altogether blameless in the matter of tampering with the secret box, Kinaringan refused to take back the creatures which had escaped, and so they remain upon earth and plague mankind to this day, a perpetual remembrance of Kabong's inquisitiveness and deceit.

As for the magic beanstalk, Kinaringan felt that Kabong was becoming rather too frequent a visitor, and therefore he caused it to wither away; so that neither Kabong nor anyone else has ever been able to make another journey to that faraway region where Kinaringan dwells beyond the clouds.

THE BEWITCHED GOAT

In one of the Borneo coast villages, whose houses stand upon posts over the water of the winding rivers, there once lived a man called Bakar the Crocodile-catcher. In the days of his youth, Bakar had a little son who was carried off by a crocodile one evening as he was playing beside the water's edge. The loss of the boy changed the whole course of Bakar's existence, for he was so distraught with grief that he determined to devote his life to the destruction of the reptiles which had been the cause of his sorrow. To that end he waged unceasing war against them. He would raid the nests in the sheltered hollows of the mangrove swamp where the females left their eggs to be hatched out by the sun; he would lie in ambush for them until they rose to the surface to sun themselves upon the river-banks, and then fling spears at them with unerring aim, and so skilled did he become in the setting and baiting of crocodile-traps that his fame spread far and wide throughout the land,

The brown people do not care to attack a crocodile unprovoked, for they fear that such an act would rouse the relatives of the slain reptile to rise in anger against them, and they dread the retaliation of enemies so powerful. But if, as often happens, one of their number is carried off, then they believe in the law of a tooth for a tooth and an eye for an eye, and do not rest until the murderer is caught and killed. Crocodiles are, however, no easy things to kill, for although you may often see them near the water's edge basking sleepily in the sunshine, so still that they look like great dark logs of wood, yet they are ever alert, and at the slightest sign of danger there is a wriggle, a flop and a splash, and they have dived beneath the friendly river.

For this reason, whenever a crocodile had to be hunted down, the villagers from far and near would call upon Bakar for his help. No hand was so cunning as his in setting the trap or preparing the bait that was to lure the enemies of mankind to their destruction. First of all he took a piece of hard wood, cut it down into a sharp stake pointed at either end and tied tightly round the middle of it a long strand of rattan. Next a white hen was caught and killed; its breast was ripped open and the sharpened stake inserted lengthways; it was then sewn up and placed in a life-like attitude on a branch of a tree which overhung the river, the long trail of rattan with a float tied to the end lying loosely upon the bank. The setting of the bait was the part of the procedure which required the greatest skill, for the wily crocodile, which has the intuition of a reptile as well as the intelligence of a mortal, is not easily taken in, and it needed many a magic spell and potent incantation before the slaughtered hen had the power to attract unfailingly, and these things Bakar had only learnt by patient experiment during the course of years.

When all was ready, there was nothing to do but wait. Sooner or later the crocodile came along. He spied the tempting mouthful above him; the charm which had been laid upon it caused him to be blinded to his danger, and so he made a snap at it with his great jaws and swallowed it whole. Thereupon the pointed stake stuck in his throat, and, infuriated by the unaccustomed pain, he made off either up or down stream as fast as he could swim. But no matter where he went, or how deeply he dived the rattan float marked his course and betrayed him, so that it was only necessary to follow it in a canoe, and, when the reptile's strength became spent, to haul him struggling to the bank and despatch him with knives and spears. On such occasions, the inmates of the whole village—men, women and children—came armed for the kill, eager to avenge the death of their friend or kinsman, and, not unmindful of the crocodile's lashing tail, they hacked him to bits, each one afterwards contributing a small gift in cash or kind to Bakar in recognition of his services.

So powerful was Bakar that the crocodiles themselves came to fear him more than they feared any mortal; they believed that by spending a lonely vigil of three days and three nights with the spirits of the jungle he had acquired the secret of invulnerability, and so could go amongst them without danger; moreover, it was said that by virtue of the brown headcloth which he wore twisted about his brows he held the secret of penetration through the river to the realm below where the crocodiles shed their reptiles' skins and assumed mortal shape.

In Bakar's village dwelt his friend Awang, who was married to a beautiful girl called Tina. One morning, Bakar was coming from his early bathe in the river, when he met Tina on the bank with a mosquito-net in her hands.

"Where are you going, Tina?" he asked.

"To the landing-stage," she answered, smiling, "and there I am going to wash this dirty old mosquito-net."

"That is surely a rash act," said Bakar, half bantering, half serious. "Do you not know the old saying, child, that one who washes a mosquito-net by the river-side will be meat for the crocodiles?"

"*Cheh,*" replied the girl, tossing her head. "Is it not true that the name of Bakar has frightened every crocodile from these reaches of the river? Why, then, should I be afraid?"

Bakar, flattered by this reference to his prowess, passed on and said no more. But when he met Awang at the market a few minutes later he told him what his wife had said.

"It is true, Bakar," said Awang, perturbed. "It is not well to trifle with the fates nor flout the wisdom of old proverbs. It is better that the net should remain dirty for all time than that my wife should risk her life in washing it. I will hasten to the river and bring her back."

Leaving the market he set off, hurrying as much as a Malay ever can hurry. As he approached the landing-stage, where it was Tina's custom to bathe and do her washing, he heard a sudden cry, followed by a splash. Alarmed at the sound, he started to run, and as he rounded the great clump of feathery bamboo which stood between the path and the bank, he was just in time to catch a glimpse of his lovely Tina being drawn beneath the river in the jaws of a gigantic crocodile. As the crocodile dived, one fair brown arm was raised above the surface of the water, and for a moment the sunlight flashed upon a golden ring that adorned the little finger of the outstretched hand. Then the water closed over it, and it was seen no more.

In vain Awang shouted; in vain he rushed waist-deep into the river and churned it into foam in hopes that the robber might drop his booty. He was too late. Only a few bubbles floating down the stream showed where his wife had vanished; only the half-washed mosquito-net, whose folds floated wanly in the water, told how she had disregarded the saying of the men of old.

Almost distracted, Awang betook himself to Bakar and sought his aid.

"We must wait," said Bakar, when he had heard his friend's sad tale. "A trap set now, however cunningly, would be of no avail. We must wait until the robber is hungry once again."

"Even if we caught him, of what help is that to me?" cried the anguished Awang, wringing his hands in distress. "Let revenge come later. It is my wife I want. Only you have the power to get her back for me, and if you will but help me before it is too late, I will gladly give you everything I possess."

"Very well," said Bakar, touched by his friend's grief, "help you I will. But only on condition that you trust me and do exactly as I tell you, even though it may be difficult."

"Any order you give me I will gladly obey," promised Awang, hope beginning to kindle in his heart.

"Then come with me and have no fear," commanded the crocodile-catcher. "But remember. Unless you obey me, all hope is lost."

He led the way to the river-bank, and, making a sign to Awang to follow him, dived into the water. Nothing daunted, Awang plunged in after him. Instead of rising to the surface again he found himself going down, down, down until at last he came with Bakar to a country which he knew must be the realm of the crocodiles. It was, as the native stories had always pictured it, a fair land like his own. On every side were smiling plains with cattle grazing, and near by was a great palace surrounded by lawns and terraces that were ablaze with the colours of ten thousand flowers and fringed with shady trees. Tied up to one of the trees was a goat, and as the two came near it they saw an old man attired in the most costly clothes approaching them.

"This is no mortal who draws near," said Bakar to Awang in an undertone, "but the King of the Crocodiles himself."

Bakar went forward, and, having saluted the King and bowed with deep respect, said:

"O Rajah, this poor man has had the misfortune to lose his wife and comes seeking her, thinking that perchance she may have wandered to this fair land of yours."

The Crocodile King looked closely at Bakar and recognised him by his brown head-cloth. Inwardly he became perturbed, for he feared Bakar's powers, and knew him to be proof against attack. But in words as suave as those in which he had been addressed he answered;

"Your friend is brave indeed to venture in such a land as this. Let him take this goat as a recognition of his courage, and return to the country whence he came."

"No," said Awang sturdily. "I have come to find my wife, and I want no goats of yours."

"Take the goat, fool," whispered Bakar in his ear, "and then let us be gone."

But Awang had forgotten his promise to do as Bakar bade

him and he said again:

"I come to find my wife. Goats I have in plenty, and of what use can this one be to me?"

"Nevertheless," persisted the King of the Crocodiles, "you had better take the goat. I offer it to you as a gift, but if you do not take it, it will be killed to-day, for this very night we celebrate a feast."

"Kill it or not," replied Awang stubbornly, paying no attention to Bakar's further whispers and warning glances, "what is that to me? I seek my wife, and do not need your goat." Then, thinking that perhaps, in his anxiety to find his beloved Tina, he had been impolite he added: "But if you will be so kind, give me then one leg; it will be enough for me, and you too will have enough for your feast to-night."

Upon hearing this, the King summoned a slave. The goat was killed, and Awang took the leg which the King gave him. Then, as Bakar told him that further search would be fruitless, he followed the crocodile-catcher sadly through the river to the upper world.

When they had reached the bank, Awang drew the goat's leg out of the water and laid it upon the grass. As he did so, to his horror and amazement it began to change its form. The long grey hair faded away, and its place was taken by light brown skin as smooth as a pearl; slowly it filled out until it became rounded and graceful, with a tiny dimple at the elbow; before his eyes the cloven hoof turned into a tiny hand, and upon the little finger of that hand he saw the gold ring he had given Tina, the wife he loved so well. Then indeed he realized how he had thrown away his happiness and Tina's life by his disregard of Bakar's warnings, and, burying his head between his hands he fell weeping upon the river-bank.

But all Bakar the Crocodile-catcher said was, "I told you so," and he went off in search of a white fowl whereby he might lure yet another of his enemies to destruction.

THE TREE OF ECHOES

Long ago, near Pontianak, in what is now Dutch Borneo, there lived a great Rajah, Abdul Hassim by name. For many years of his married life he had no children, and this was a great sorrow to him, since he longed to have a son who might succeed him upon the throne of ancestors. At last, however, his prayers were heard, and the Ranee, his wife, gave birth to twins.

They were two boys, these twins; but on the very night of their arrival into the world, one of them vanished mysteriously from the royal palace. A hue and cry was raised, the royal apartments were searched, and all the Rajah's retinue were questioned; parties were sent out to scour the jungle and the surrounding villages, but no trace of the missing baby could be found.

Towards dawn, the Rajah, weary and sick with disappointment, flung himself upon a mat-covered divan in his chamber and fell asleep. As he slept he dreamt that he was wandering along an unfrequented path in the jungle. On every side rose giants of the forest, their branches far above him making a network of leaves so dense that he could catch only tiny glimpses of the sky. It was evening, and suddenly in the half-light a strange being dropped from one of the lower boughs of a great camphor tree, drew itself up and confronted him on the path. The Rajah shuddered and drew back in fear, for he saw that he was in the presence of one of the dreaded goblins of the jungle, which have powers unknown to the human race. Its stature was greater than a mortal's; its fingers were as long as the tails of lizards, and its ears stood like a stag's, while its great eyes shone like burnished brass. It regarded the Rajah steadfastly for a moment, barring his way; then, in a voice as deep as the grunting of a pig, it said:

"O Rajah, your son is become the spirit of the banyan-tree!"

Having spoken thus the goblin vanished, although, in his dream, the Rajah tried to stay its going, in order to ask the meaning of its strange words. When he awoke, he remembered his dream very vividly and since, like all his people, he had the greatest respect for visions and for the supernatural, he did not dismiss it from his mind as the outcome of his fevered imagination. Rather, he turned the saying of the goblin over in his mind, but the more he pondered, the more was he at a loss to understand its meaning, particularly as there was, in those days, no banyan-tree near the royal palace. Nevertheless, he commanded the search-parties to go out again and hunt through all the jungle until they found a banyan-tree. It was a forlorn hope, but he thought that, in this way, they might find some trace of his missing son.

Now the banyan is one tree above all others that is feared by the brown people. It is a tree of mystery, gnarled, with hanging roots and densely spreading branches which cast deep shadows; the fitting abode of the evil spirits which haunt its precincts, and wait to twine bony fingers round the throats of any passer-by foolhardy enough to linger beneath its gloomy boughs. There was no likelihood of the search-parties overlooking such a tree had they but come upon one, yet all their labour was in vain, and, although they roamed the forests until the shades of night were falling, they found no banyan-tree, much less any trace of the baby prince.

The next morning, as the sun was rising above the rippling line of hill-tops, Rajah Abdul Hassim was walking in his palace garden disconsolate and heavy-hearted, for the son who was lost seemed to him more precious even than the one who was sleeping safely in the Ranee's arms.

As he paced to and fro, deep in thought, he came to the centre of a grassy lawn that spread out before the palace down to the river-bank. Neither tree nor shrub had ever been planted there, and all at once the Rajah stopped in his walk for, in the middle of the lawn, where nothing had been before, a young sapling was shooting out its leaves. As the Rajah bent down to examine it a sudden wonder gripped his heart. Quickly he summoned the palace gardeners to the spot and questioned them as to what manner of tree the sapling was, and each one of them, after long inspection, averred that it was what no living man had ever seen before, a seedling banyan-tree. It was a marvel, said they, for banyan-trees are like aged men: to those who know them they seem so old that they can never have had a youth.

But banyan it was, and as the Rajah's son grew big and strong within the palace so flourished the tree, growing greater every day as no other tree in all that land had ever been known to grow before. Day by day it put out new branches, day by day it sent forth a fresh abundance of its strange hanging roots. This alone was enough for men to realize that it was no ordinary tree. Nor was that all. There was something even more uncanny about this tree of mystery. When the royal baby in the palace cried, the banyan, even on days when there was not enough wind to stir a leaf, would wave its branches to and fro, and from their depths would come an answering cry; when the babe laughed the voice within the banyan would laugh too, and later, when the boy learnt to talk, strange mutterings would be heard issuing from the tree, and, at times of feasts and festivals, the sound of drums and of booming gongs. It was a tree of echoes.

No one dared to venture near the banyan, which continued to grow greater every day, but the sounds which came from it could be heard in the royal palace, disquieting the whole household, and the Rajah most of all.

At last, after deep thought, the Rajah summoned his chief minister to a private conclave.

"We live beneath the shadow of a terror, O Bandahara," he said, "and the people become troubled and fear that disaster will come upon the land. Were it well, think you, to hew down this ill-omened tree?"

"Indeed, Your Highness," replied the Bandahara, "it seems to me that there can be no other way, if we are to silence that strange spirit which dwells within."

Accordingly the Rajah, though not without trepidation, gave the order that the banyan should be felled, hoping that in this way he might give peace to the spirit of his twin son who abode within, and at the same time still the nameless fears that beset his people.

First of all the royal gardeners were called, but although they hewed with a will, eager to be done with so sinister a task, they could make little impression upon the great gnarled trunks. They wrought till the sun was setting, and as they wended their way homewards they said:

"To-morrow will see the ending of our toil, and the giant will come crashing to the ground."

But when the morrow came all were amazed to see that, during the night, every wound had healed, and that the tree showed not a sign of an axe's mark.

After that, all the most noted woodmen in the Rajah's realm were called, men versed in every kind of jungle lore; but, although they hewed all day long until the setting of the sun, they could never bring the great tree to earth, and by dawn all its wounds were healed. Nor, in spite of the promise of rich rewards, could a man be found stout-hearted enough to stay beneath its mysterious branches once the sun had set.

And so the years went by, and still the banyan remained, growing in size and stature even as the Rajah's son. All day and all night long strange sounds and echoes came from its depths, and it increased to such girth and spread as never had been beheld, with a score of trunks and a thousand branches, while its creepers hung from it like an old man's beard.

At length, Rajah Abdul Hassim, worn-out with anxiety and

disappointment, passed away and was succeeded by his son. On the morning of the festival of the young prince's coming to the throne, the banyan-tree was seen to have grown almost double its vast size, and, during the feast, the sound of gongs and drums and laughter came from it even more loudly than had ever been heard before.

The young Rajah, who had always hated and feared the tree, became more and more perturbed, for he could think of no way in which he might rid himself of the remembrance of his spirit brother. At last one night, as he lay tossing restlessly upon his mats, he too dreamt that he was walking through the jungle, and the goblin of the jungle appeared to him in his dream, just as it had appeared to his father many years before. Its fingers were as long as the tails of lizards, and its ears stood like a stag's, while its great eyes shone like burnished brass. Then, in a voice as deep as the grunting of a pig, the young Rajah seemed to hear it say:

"Axes of iron are of no avail, but the Tree of Echoes will yield to an axehead made of tin. Give forth this news, O Rajah, to your people, and if in your realm there be one stout enough of heart to fell the tree with such an axe, to him and his shall be given the power of coming to life again after they have been buried in the grave."

As soon as he awoke the young Rajah, with the words of the goblin ringing in his ears, gave orders that an axehead of tin should be made without delay. But, when it had been fashioned, not a man could be found of sufficient courage to attack the banyan-tree, so great an object of awe was it become. Vain were the promises of rewards, futile the threats of punishment. To those who dwelt near the shadow of the tree the fear of the vengeance that the banyan spirit might wreak upon one who destroyed its haunts outweighed rewards, and made human threats of small account. Not one of the Rajah's subjects would lay a finger upon the tree, much as they would have loved to see it lying prostrate upon the ground.

The Rajah and his ministers were in despair, when one day there came to the palace craving audience a young man dressed in rags.

"Your Highness," said he, prostrating himself before the throne, "my name is Suliman. I am come from the far-away village of Matan, whither the news of your proclamation has but lately penetrated. A long drought has destroyed our crops and we are upon the verge of famine; in fact, so poor and wretched am I become that I feel that no evil spirit can reduce me to a plight worse than that in which I am already. Therefore I have come to tell you that I am ready to try the axe of tin upon the enchanted tree."

The Rajah was overjoyed to find that there was after all one man in his dominions willing to pit himself against the banyan, and he commanded that the axe of tin should be given to Suliman without delay.

Suliman took it and tried its edge. Then he drew it back over his shoulder and aimed a mighty blow at the banyan's trunk. To the amazement of all, the axehead bit into the tree, which offered no resistance to the shower of blows that followed, and the great trunks were severed as though they were nothing more substantial than bamboo. It was but a few minutes before the giant came crashing to the ground, with the noise of a thousand thunders. As it fell, they say there arose from somewhere amidst its branches one great despairing cry which turned the watchers' hearts to stone. Afterwards all was silent and the spirit of the tree was never heard again.

But to this day the people of Matan, Suliman's village, are known to return from the graves in which they have been buried, even as the goblin of the forest had foretold. For forty days they wander in their human forms, and you may know them, it is said, by the earthy smell which clings about their clothes. Then, after their brief spell of resurrection, they are seen no more.

The Vengeance of the Bog

One of the smiling plains of Borneo there rises, like an island from the midst of a green sea, a strangely shaped hill called Rindihan. It is covered with long grass, and looks as though it were the mound of a vast grave. And that is exactly what the brown people, who dwell near by, believe it is —the grave, not of one person nor yet of a mighty giant, but of a whole village.

In olden days, the ground where Rindihan Hill now stands was flat, and the site of a prosperous settlement. This village was not a collection of little houses, but consisted of one long building over two hundred feet in length, in which dwelt a whole community; for those were the days of head-hunters, and there was safety in numbers.

Head-hunting feuds began with a conflict between private individuals, and gradually developed into a war between villages, until life became so insecure that no one dared to go about his business save in parties of considerable numbers. For this reason the inhabitants of Rindihan herded together in one long house. The walls of the building were made of tree bark flattened out in long strips, the roof was thatched with palm-leaves, and the floor was made of split bamboo. The whole house was raised on posts several feet from the ground and reached by a log laid slanting towards the entrance, with notches cut in it to serve as steps. The doors at either end could be closed at night or in times of danger, but each had a small hole cut in the base to allow the village dogs to come to and fro as they listed. Within, the space was divided into cubicles in each of which lived a family, whilst a wide verandah ran the length of the house. The eaves came down within a few feet of the floor.

It had never occurred to the architects that chimneys and windows would be desirable, and the smoke from each little hearth had to escape as best it could, so that roof and rafters gleamed black with the grime of ages. Below the darkened roof was a kind of ceiling where the treasures of the villagers were stored away: old jars—most precious of their possessions; fishing-nets and fish-traps; blowpipes and spears; rice-bins, game snares and old buffalo-horns, all jumbled together in confusion. In every little cubicle hung the family fetish, a collection of animals' teeth, beads, bells, deer-hooves, and oddly shaped beans and stones bound together, a potent charm to ward off sickness and disaster, while from the rafters dangled, for all the world like so many coconuts, a cluster of smoked human skulls, grinning horribly, a boar's tusk in the hole where the nose had been putting a finishing touch of the grotesque to their appearance. Underneath the house was the village pig-sty; fowls, dogs and babies roamed everywhere; outside the door, in a hive made of tree-bark, was a swarm of bees; hanging from the eaves were round cages containing tiny birds of bright green plumage, while to a post was tied a tame monkey. For, though the inmates of the village were head-hunters, they were fond of pets.

Here it was that the men of Rindihan, under their chief, Rundai, kept perpetual watch for hostile raiding-parties. Even the beaks of the cocks were tied up at night to prevent their giving away the position of the village in the darkness, and any one who had *kurap,* a skin disease prevalent among the brown people, which sets up constant irritation, used to make a good thing out of it by selling it to heavy sleepers, for its possession ensured wakefulness, and wakefulness was necessary if lives and property were to be protected.

Although Rundai and his people went in constant fear of attack themselves, they did not scruple to attack others if the opportunity arose. The young bloods were not counted men until they had been tattooed, an operation they could not have performed until they had secured their first head. Moreover, the village maidens looked askance at a lover, no matter how presentable and ardent he might be, if he had not laid at least one grisly trophy at her feet.

At the same time, the Rindihans did not collect heads purely as a hobby, like small boys collect butterflies, and they only attacked villages with which they had a definite feud. One of these feuds was with the men of Wasai, a village perched upon a hill several days' march away. The feud was started on a day when Rundai met Binas, the chief of Wasai, and had a difference of opinion with him over the payment of the price of a buffalo. There was a quarrel. Both chiefs lost their tempers, but before his opponent could take the offensive, Rundai drew his long sword from its sheath, and, with one sweeping blow, severed the head of Binas from his body. The head rolled away into the jungle, and Rundai, darting after it, seized it by its long hair and bore it back in triumph to Rindihan.

It was not long before the men of Wasai discovered the headless body of their chief in the jungle, and they soon found out who his assailant had been. At once there was a call to arms. A raid was planned. A band of seven avengers arrayed themselves in full war-dress and sallied forth towards Rindihan, intent upon obtaining retribution for the slaying of their chief.

When they had gone one day's march upon their journey, and were wending their way in single file along the jungle track, a deer burst out of the undergrowth, barking sharply, dashed across the path and was lost to sight. This was the most evil of omens, and, knowing that the expedition could meet with nothing but disaster if they went forward, they retraced their steps to Wasai. They waited in the village until ten days had passed and then set out again. They had been gone three days upon the second journey when a bird flew out of a forest tree in front of them uttering a shrill call. This was an omen no less serious than the barking of the deer, and again they returned home for ten days.

On the third journey, however, they met with no evil omens and without adventure reached the great clearing where the people of Rindihan were planting their rice. As they lurked round the outskirts of the village they could see no sign of Rundai himself; but to them that mattered not at all, for, as evening drew on, they spied two old women returning from the stream with water in their long bamboos. Like a flash the raiders leapt upon them, and, before they had time even to scream, severed their heads and returned to Wasai, where they became the heroes of the day.

Rundai and his people could not lie down under such a defeat. They bided their time. Then one morning Rundai called his lieutenants to him.

"The time is come," said he, "to consult the omens. Let us inspect the liver of a pig."

Straightway a pig was caught and slaughtered before the house. Its liver was healthy and without a blemish. The wise men cried that a raid would be successful if it were made without delay.

"It is well," said Rundai. "Now shall the dogs of Wasai feel the might of the avenger's hand."

As it chanced, the next day a market was being held near the coast. Rundai and his people made an ambush in the dense undergrowth beside the path, and, lying in wait, cut off a party of Wasai men as they went past, laden with great loads of wild rubber they had collected in the forest. Seven heads fell into the Rindihans' hands, a harvest greater than any they had ever reaped before. The fate of the old women was avenged.

As they approached the village, shouting and singing in triumph, Rundai turned to his comrades and held up a warning finger.

"Friends," he said in an undertone, "it were well to go quietly. We draw near the dwelling of the Bog, and, hating all clamour as he does, we had best not disturb him, lest we rouse him to slay us with that sword-like tongue of his."

At this the party became silent, for the Bog, whose existence they had forgotten in the moment of their exultation, was a greater menace to the men of Rindihan than any head-hunter. He was a strange misshapen monster with a tongue like a wavy Malayan sword, and dwelt in a gloomy cavern that ran far down into the earth. If left in peace he did no harm, but if any passed near by his haunt laughing or singing, or—worst of all—beating a drum, he would become distracted with rage, and would chase the offender through the jungle. In vain would it be for the fugitive to seek refuge by climbing a tree, for so sharp was the Bog's tongue that he could cut through the stoutest trunk, or, if the fancy pleased him, he would summon his numerous progeny from the cavern and climb upon their backs so that he could reach the offending mortal. He was the enemy of animals no less than of men if the former disturbed him, but the monkeys had special privileges, for them he looked upon as his friends.

So Rundai and his party went stealthily until they had passed the dwelling of the dreaded Bog. But once they reached the village the excitement of their homecoming was so great, and their reception so enthusiastic, that prudence was forgotten. Preparations for a great feast were made, and Rundai, who had long been experimenting in the making of gongs, thought that it would be a suitable occasion to bring them forth and test their tones.

"I fear the Bog, husband," said his wife anxiously. "You know well that for years no drum has been beaten in the village lest we should arouse his wrath; the sound of these gongs of yours will surely reach him, and if he is disturbed, who knows what disaster may not come upon us?"

But Rundai had forgotten the fears which had beset him earlier in the day. It was his hour of triumph, and he was determined that his victory should be celebrated with fitting pomp.

"The wind is from the hills," he answered reassuringly. "It will carry the sound of the gongs away to the sea, and the Bog will sleep in peace."

So preparations for the feast went forward. A buffalo was slaughtered and jars of coconut-toddy were produced. Rundai's great brass gongs were ranged in a row on the long verandah of the village house. Taking a piece of wood, Rundai began to beat them, and soon the night was filled with their deep-toned booming, and with the thunder of the drums which accompanied the music. As the night wore on, the libations of coconut-toddy were passed more frequently from hand to hand in the long bamboo tubes. Men's hearts grew warm; long came the bursts of laughter, heavy the stamp of dancing feet, and shrill rose the voices as they sang the chant of victory. The feast grew more riotous, and the music of the gongs floated over the plain more loudly than before.

When the excitement was at its height, Rundai caught sight of the village monkey, which was chattering upon its post. Laughing boisterously, he seized it and bore it off to his family cubicle, where he dressed it up in a shirt belonging to his little son, and set a raiding-hat gay with cock's feathers upon its head.

"See, my friends! Another merrymaker comes to join our feast!" he cried. With that he led the monkey out into the verandah, and holding it by its fore-paws began to dance with it.

A great shout of laughter went up from all assembled, and they became convulsed with mirth as they beheld their chief prancing round with his chattering partner, while those who beat the gongs redoubled their energies, heedless for once of that dread monster who befriended monkeys and hated clamour of any kind.

But the unaccustomed booming of Rundai's gongs had

The outraged Bog shambled through the jungle.

already roused the Bog from his slumbers. For a while he listened, his anger gathering like a storm. Through the still night air the sounds came louder and yet louder to his cavern in the earth—the shouts of laughter, the chanting voices, the stamp of dancing feet, the thundering drums, and, worse than all of these, the eternal booming of the gongs. Then suddenly he heard one sound rise shrilly above the others. It was the screech of a frightened monkey.

The outraged Bog arose from his lair, and, calling his offspring, he shambled through the jungle towards the village of Rindihan, passing without heed a little band of men, who cowered aside in the bushes as he went by. With his tongue that was wavy like a Malayan sword, and as sharp as its edge, he cut through the posts on which the long building stood raised from the ground as though they were but reeds, and as house and everything it contained came crashing without warning to the ground, he cried aloud:

"Such, O Rundai, is the fate of beaters of gongs and taunters of monkeys!"

Not content with the destruction he had wrought, the Bog and his progeny set to, and, digging into the ground with their long talons, buried the whole village with Rundai and his people and all his gongs beneath the great mound of earth which is called Rindihan Hill, so that not one escaped, not one, that is, but the monkey whose cause the Bog had championed with his own.

Thus it was that, when the little party of men whom the Bog had passed unheedingly in the jungle—in fact no others than an avenging band from Wasai—reached the spot as the dawn was breaking, they found not a trace of the village left. But as they stood gazing wide-eyed with amazement, there came to their wondering ears the faint music of distant gongs ascending from the depths of the newly risen hill. Terror-stricken and baulked of retaliation for the death of their comrades, they fled with the story to their homes.

It is long since the Bog and all his race departed to a land where neither drum, nor booming gong nor other noise has power to disquiet; but to this day the brown people, although they have taken to beating gongs again, fear to make mock of a monkey, mindful of the fate of Rundai and his men and dreading that the sleeping spirit of the Bog might be roused to wrath once more, and bring upon their heads swift retribution.

And they say that even now, if you care to linger near those grassy slopes on a calm night, you may still hear the booming of Rundai's gongs coming faintly but melodiously from the bosom of Rindihan Hill.

Other titles by *Natural History Publications (Borneo)*

For more information, please contact us at

Natural History Publications (Borneo) Sdn. Bhd.
A913, 9th Floor, Wisma Merdeka
P.O. Box 13908, 88846 Kota Kinabalu, Sabah, Malaysia
Tel: 088-233098   Fax: 088-240768   e-mail: chewlun@tm.net.my

Mount Kinabalu: Borneo's Magic Moutain—an introduction to the natural history of one of the world's great natural monuments *by* K.M. Wong & C.L. Chan

Enchanted Gardens of Kinabalu: A Borneo Diary *by* Susan M. Phillipps

A Colour Guide to Kinabalu Park *by* Susan K. Jacobson

Kinabalu: The Haunted Mountain of Borneo *by* C.M. Enriquez (Reprint)

A Walk through the Lowland Rainforest of Sabah *by* Elaine J.F. Campbell

In Brunei Forests: An Introduction to the Plant Life of Brunei Darussalam *by* K.M. Wong (Revised edition)

The Larger Fungi of Borneo by David N. Pegler

Pitcher-plants of Borneo *by* Anthea Phillipps & Anthony Lamb

Nepenthes of Borneo *by* Charles Clarke

The Plants of Mount Kinabalu 3: Gymnosperms and Non-orchid Monocotyledons by John H. Beaman & Reed S. Beaman

Slipper Orchids of Borneo *by* Phillip Cribb

The Genus paphiopedilum (Second Edition) *by* Phillip Cribb

Gingers of Peninsular Malaysia and Singapore by K. Larsen, H. Ibrahim, S.H. Khaw & L.G. Saw

Mosses and Liverworts of Mount Kinabalu *by* Jan P. Frahm, Wolfgang Frey, Harald Kürschner & Mario Manzel

Birds of Mount Kinabalu, Borneo *by* Geoffrey W.H. Davison

Proboscis Monkeys of Borneo *by* Elizabeth L. Bennett & Francis Gombek

The Natural History of Orang-utan *by* Elizabeth L. Bennett

The Systematics and Zoogeography of the Amphibia of Borneo *by* Robert F. Inger (Reprint)

A Field Guide to the Frogs of Borneo *by* Robert F. Inger & Robert B. Stuebing

The Natural History of Amphibians and Reptiles in Sabah *by* Robert F. Inger & Tan Fui Lian

A Field Guide to the Snakes of Borneo *by* Robert B. Stuebing & Robert F. Inger

Marine Food Fishes and Fisheries of Sabah *by* Chin Phui Kong

Land Below the Wind *by* Agnes N. Keith (Reprint)

Three Came Home *by* Agnes N. Keith (Reprint)

An Introduction to the Traditional Costumes of Sabah (*eds.* Rita Lasimbang & Stella Moo-Tan)

Manual latihan pemuliharaan dan penyelidikan hidupan liar di lapangan *by* Alan Rabinowitz (*Translated by* Maryati Mohamed)

Ethnobotani *by* Gary Martin (*Translated by* Maryati Mohamed)